FOUNDATIONS OF MODERN HISTORY

General Editor: A. Goodwin

Emeritus Professor of Modern History, University of Manchester

By the same author:

ENGLISH PUBLIC DEBT IN THE EIGHTEENTH CENTURY (1968)
DUTCH REPUBLIC IN EUROPE IN THE SEVEN YEARS WAR (1971)

Neutrality or Commitment:

The Evolution of Dutch Foreign Policy, 1667–1795

by
ALICE CLARE CARTER

Senior Lecturer in History, London School of Economics and Political Science

EDWARD ARNOLD

General Preface

Mrs Carter's scholarly analysis of the complex motivation of the Dutch Republic's foreign policy from the age of Louis XIV to the French revolution fills an important gap in the history of international relations in the eighteenth century. It shows that contemporary European diplomatists who tended to exaggerate the potential role of the United Provinces in the Great Power rivalry at this period and modern historians who have under-valued it were both at fault in assuming that by then the Netherlands had forfeited all chance of pursuing an independent line in foreign policy. There has thus been considerable misunderstanding of the continuing Dutch need to steer a middle course between the policy of commitment and that of unarmed neutrality. In times of crisis foreign alliances were often dictated by the imperative needs of national security but even when the Great Powers were at war and Dutch interests were not vitally concerned, the alternative policy of non-alignment seemed to the Dutch preferable in order to preserve and promote their profitable carrying trade and to resolve, if possible, the friction between the pro- and anti-Stadholderian factions in the divided and vulnerable Republic.

During the greater part of the eighteenth century, when the seeds of the Republic's economic decline had been sown but had not yet fully matured, the twin bases of its foreign policy were, in fact, the so-called Barrier policy of maintaining guaranteed military positions garrisioned by the Dutch along the borders of the Southern Netherlands against actual or potential French aggression and the trade-oriented policy of neutrality in the European and colonial conflicts between France and Britain. Both of these preoccupations had stemmed from the second and third Anglo-Dutch wars and from the forty years' struggle with the France of Louis XIV. Mrs. Carter's account of the remoter origins of the Barrier policy and of the Anglo-Dutch commercial agreement of 1674 and the Anglo-Dutch defensive treaty of 1678 provides the key to the understanding of how the Dutch were able to implement their via media in foreign policy during later periods of intermittent European stability and international and colonial warfare.

The momentous contribution of the Dutch to the checkmating of French aggression under Louis XIV is well known. Less clearly recognized, however, are their subsequent achievements in helping to preserve the English Protestant Succession against the Catholic Jacobite menace, the successful defence of their eastern as well as their southern frontiers, and the maintenance, until the last decades of the eighteenth century, of the independence of their external policy from foreign domination.

Much of the interest of Mrs. Carter's study of Dutch foreign policy at this period derives from her intimate knowledge of the complexities of the decision-making process within the federal Republic and her sympathetic understanding of the domestic difficulties – constitutional, financial, and dynastic – which perplexed its rulers and inhibited their freedom of action. This book is thus a real contribution not only to the detailed study of Dutch foreign relations but also to the understanding of the social, political and intellectual trends in the United Provinces in the pre-revolutionary period. Not the least of its merits is that its conclusions are solidly based on Dutch state and municipal records and on the author's own critical evaluation of the latest trends in Dutch historical scholarship.

A. GOODWIN

Maps

Contents

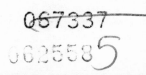

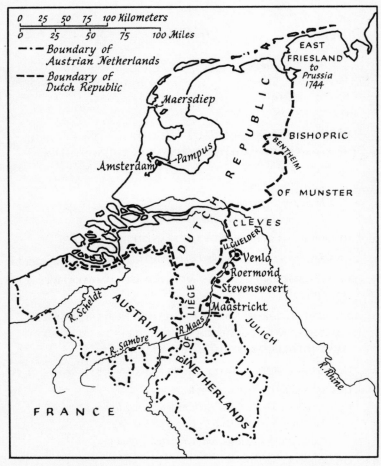

The Dutch Republic and the Austrian Netherlands in the Eighteenth Century

Introduction

IN the seventeenth century the Dutch Republic was acknowledged to be among the major powers of Europe. But it hardly owed this pre-eminence to its geographical location. To the north and the west it was barely free of the sea; much inland territory was under water, and vast resources of man-power and money were then, and in modern times are still, needed to combat this menace to its very existence. To the east, except for some way along the lower reaches of the River Ems, the Republic was without clear demarcation of its territory. Brandenburg–Prussia and the predatory prelates of Munster and Cologne took advantage of this weakness at their convenience. To the south there had once been frontier lines along the major delta mouths of the River Rhine. Once the Spaniards had been pushed back by Dutch armies, however, the frontier with the Southern Netherlands was, and indeed with Belgium remains, entirely illogical. Dutch children learn at school that politics and war, not nature, drew their native frontiers.

How then did this small country, water-logged, water-threatened, unblessed with clearly-drawn frontiers and moreover with a relatively small population, estimated at just over 1 million, which it could not supply with home-grown grain, achieve its seventeenth-century preeminence? The answer lies less in domestic than in exterior circumstances. But before we try to find it, there are some basic facts about the Dutch Republic which can never be overstressed and must be kept in mind. The three seaboard provinces of the seven which between them made up the Republic, were then, and one of them still is, the richest and most populous of all. Holland itself contributed nearly 60 per cent of the revenue of the Union. Within this province was Amsterdam, itself contributing over 50 per cent of the revenue of the province of Holland. Much of the wealth of Amsterdam, and its phenomenal rise to the position of the major seaport of Western Europe was attributable to external circumstances such as the intense preoccupation of neighbouring countries, especially England, with their own internal problems in

the period of the city's most rapid growth, between 1620 and 1650.
Also significant was the increasing size of the navies of the maritime
countries in a period when the skills of naval architects were
enabling larger and larger ships to be built. We must also take into
account the demographic factor of Amsterdam's urban population,
swollen by the drift of victims of religious persecution to a city
where toleration flourished and a ready market for their industrial
skills was available. According to tradition, Amsterdam's growth
was based on the herring industry. But other pillars were Baltic grain
and its partner, ship-timbers for western Europe's growing navies.
From supplying Europe's dockyards with timber, and shipping
North Germany's grain to wherever it was needed, even to the
Mediterranean, it was but a short step to acquiring the major share
of all Europe's coast-wise trade. When we add to this supreme
technical skills in ship-design and building, especially the so-called
'fly-boat,' specially built to accommodate different cargoes, we can
see why this virtually defenceless and not over-productive small
country played for a while a vital role in seventeenth-century
Europe. Since Dutch seamen were the greatest explorers, and their
employers, the merchants who controlled the trading companies,
were the most successful exploiters of exotic and much sought-after
cargoes from the Far East and for a time of the Far West, there is no
need to wonder at the richness of the Dutch Republic in its Golden
Age.

How should a small, essentially disunited political
agglomeration, lacking logical frontiers yet with great wealth got by
discharging essential functions in European trade, regard itself in
relation to its neighbours? The compelling need for independence
from Spain had been achieved by 1609, long before the fact was
officially recognized in the Treaty of Munster in 1648. But the
struggle to achieve independence had been hard and had entailed
severe sacrifices for all of the Republic's seven constituent
provinces. Control of the army of the so-called 'Generality' had, of
necessity, to be surrendered to some central authority. Not
unnaturally, in view of the history of the earlier revolt, that
authority was the ruling member of the House of Orange,
descendants and collaterals of the heroic William the Silent. By
mid-seventeenth century this house, already possessed through its
Orange principality in France, of what seventeenth-century
opinion valued above all, the rights of sovereignty, had become
dynastically involved with the Bourbon-allied Stuarts in England

and with the rising Hohenzollerns, electoral rulers of Brandenburg. Sovereign rights were objectionable to the wealthy merchant oligarchs, especially of the Northern Netherlands where the earlier revolt had marked the climax of reaction against attempts to establish just such rights in face of customary local liberties. Above all sovereign rights, except *soi-disant* of its own town governors, were abhorred by wealthy Amsterdam, major support of the Orange-led army victorious in 1648. As soon as peace was made, the Amsterdammers had tried to get the army reduced. The Orange head, William II, refused: his royal connections, his life-style, the ambitions of his Prussian mother, all seemed to point towards a desire for a dynasty with sovereign rights in the Netherlands themselves. When in 1650 William II was rash enough to attempt a coup d'état against Amsterdam itself, to induce its leaders to withdraw their demands for demobilization of the Dutch army, these fears seemed to be confirmed. William was obliged to give way but memories, always long in the Republic, lingered on. When shortly afterwards the young Stadholder died, there were public rejoicings in Amsterdam. On William II's death, his English widow was pregnant with the future Stadholder-King, William III. The Republic, having achieved titular as well as actual freedom from Spain, could dispense with the House of Orange and the expense of an army, always in peace-time an apparent luxury. The Amsterdammers, who had carried much of the costs of war, now diverted their funds into trade and its protection. The dynastically threatening Stadholderate could be allowed to sink into the background. A more truly republican, so-called Stadholderless regime ensued; and the Republic's place in Europe could be redefined. The way seemed clear ahead for a policy based on the interests of Dutch trade, with only an occasional backward look at the security of the immediate frontiers.

It is important to realize that Dutch policy in Europe was never dominated by hopes of territorial conquest. Even Dutch attempts to gain a foothold in the Southern Netherlands – the policy of the later so-called Barrier System – were caused by desire not for expansion but for security. Security to the south was threatened because of the expansionist aims of France, a power the Republic was traditionally anxious to have as a friend but not as a neighbour. The Southern Netherlands, controlled by the declining forces of Spain, were earlier regarded by Dutch statesmen as a *scheidingszone* or buffer state. If we talk about a 'barrier' policy before the Spanish

Succession War we must be careful to avoid using a capital letter. It was only during the Forty Years War with France, which lasted off and on from 1672 until 1715, that there gradually evolved the concept of a line of fortified places between the French northern frontier and the Southern Netherlands. And the Republic would have been happy had it been possible to acquire a similar buffer state to the east. For on most occasions attack threatened, not by way of the Southern Netherlands, but by way of the Rhine and the Maas. Always the overriding motive in Dutch policy towards Europe was security and peace. Except when they threatened Dutch trade, or her peace and security, events in Europe did not determine the Republic's policy. They can rather be said to have distorted it.

Before we can fully appreciate Dutch foreign policy, we must try to grasp the complicated system by which it was implemented, and realize how politically vulnerable it was. The grand pensionary of Holland, the most important permanent official of by far the most powerful province, was often regarded by foreign representatives at The Hague as equivalent to a minister for external affairs. But his importance derived from his power in his own provincial states, not from any status he enjoyed as a representative of the loose federation known as the States-General. Officially the control of Dutch foreign policy was vested in the States-General by virtue of powers delegated to it by the separate sovereign provincial states. By mid-seventeenth century, however, the Secret Committee of the States-General perused reports received from Dutch representatives abroad, drew up instructions for them and recommended action to its parent body, under the oversight of an official whose title was that of greffier, literally clerk-record-keeper.

The trouble with such a system was that the provincial delegates to the States-General were not provided with powers to act in emergency without specific instructions. This meant that even matters requiring immediate action had to be reported back to provincial states' meetings. From there, as the nobility and town delegates to the provincial states were also insufficiently empowered to act without definite instructions, they had to go to their own assemblies, where the proceedings could seldom be kept absolutely confidential. There was thus no speed, and little secrecy about the official conduct of Dutch foreign policy.

But the more or less permanent residence of the grand pensionary of the States of Holland in The Hague itself provided a short cut to the centre of the Republic's foreign service. This was especially so when the office was held, as it was in 1667, by as strong, and as capable, a statesman as John de Witt. By the end of the Second Anglo-Dutch war de Witt was generally in control of Dutch foreign policy, and was so regarded abroad. Indeed no foreign ambassadors to the States would dare to disregard a holder of this key office. Grand pensionaries gave audience in the style of principal ministers for foreign affairs, and conducted their own correspondence with Dutch ambassadors abroad. This correspondence is often more informative, as well as more interesting, than the dispatches to or from the greffier, who kept official papers and reported to the Secret Committee of the States-General. Of course this official was also closely involved in the conduct of Dutch foreign policy; especially when the greffier was a strong, decisive or even merely eccentric individual his influence could be important. Foreign observers soon came to realize that the relations between the grand pensionary and the greffier were of vital importance to the success of whatever business they might have in hand. Later still, it was to become clear that in the Republic the only way to get things done was to seek out and attempt to influence someone who was strong and determined enough to circumvent accepted methods of procedure. And presently these became obscured.[1]

How did the Republic stand in Europe when the Treaty of Breda concluded the second Anglo-Dutch war? Jones calls the treaty a 'compromise',[2] explaining that this had to be so because of the war breaking out in the Southern Netherlands between Spain and Louis XIV, apparently keen to see right done to his Spanish queen in the matter of her inheritance but really, as was soon perceived, out for what he could get. The fact is that even as early as 1667, although an earlier French alliance of 1662 had seemed not to serve the Republic badly, in view of the apparent approaching break-up of the Spanish royal line, fears for the Republic's future safety were beginning to loom larger than concern for the betterment of her trade, for which the previous Anglo-Dutch wars had been fought. All the same, thanks to the brilliant Dutch naval expedition by which in June 1667 England's fleet was attacked within the waters of the Thames

---

[1] On Dutch procedures in the conduct of foreign affairs, see M. A. M. Franken, 'General tendencies and structural aspects of the foreign policy and diplomacy of the Dutch Republic', *Acta Historiae Neerlandica III*, esp. 19–42, and R. M. Hatton, *Diplomatic relations between Great Britain and the Dutch Republic* (1950), 21–3.

[2] J. R. Jones, *Britain and Europe in the Seventeenth Century* (1966), 60.

itself, the Republic did quite well out of the treaty and her European image was improved even to the point of her being courted by France. A balance was arrived at between English and Dutch aspirations for colonial trade. The English position was favoured in Africa, 'New Amsterdam' became 'New York', much to the satisfaction of the Dutch West India Company, which shed an expensive liability, whilst the Dutch gained potentially useful Surinam, and Pulo-Run in the East Indies. In other ways the Dutch were also winners, for in 1668 the 'free ships, free goods' principle, always a major Dutch objective, was recognized by England; and the definition of what constituted contraband of war was narrowed in accordance with Dutch desires to include only actual weapons.[3]

Although the 1667 treaty and its sequel appeared to bring the Dutch advantages, there were some ill-effects of the war. Among these was the transfer during its course of large numbers of Dutch fly-boats to the English mercantile marine as prizes. As the English were already beginning to impair the Dutch lead in the field of Europe's carrying trade, this seriously unbalanced the previous equation between the two fleets. Although the Dutch could and did still build ships quickly, the English merchant marine became stronger during and after the war than it had been previously, in spite of its own considerable losses and in spite of the poverty of the English crown. Indeed it is arguable that the end of the second Anglo-Dutch war marks the downturn of the Republic's prosperity, and that thereafter, with the threats to its security, and conditions becoming less favourable to its trade, the long drawn-out process of decline got under way. It is for these reasons that 1667 has been chosen as the starting point of this survey.

[3] P. C. Jessup and F. Deake, *Neutrality, its history, economics and law* I (New York, 1935–6), 35ff.

CHAPTER ONE

The Search for Security to the South

THE period between the death of William in 1650, and the appointment of his son as Stadholder with full powers in 1672, is generally known in Dutch history as the first Stadholderless regime. In these years the Republic found security in the south owing to the weakness of Spain, a rapprochement with France, with which de Witt negotiated a treaty in 1662, and as time went on, the unpreparedness of France to go over to attack in the Southern Netherlands. This is not to say that de Witt had been unmindful of danger threatening from this weak but internationally desirable and essentially wealthy neighbouring area. The main Dutch preoccupation, loudly echoing English merchants' fears of the former trading Colossus, Antwerp, had long been to maintain control over traffic proceeding by the mouth of the River Scheldt. Since the Netherlanders had been able to span the Scheldt estuary, they had set up higher and higher tariff barriers which in time effectively cut Antwerp off from the sea.[1] The trade of Amsterdam, not to speak of that of London and of some of the English outports, had thereby been greatly advantaged. The principal sufferers, Spain and her unfortunate subjects in the Southern Netherlands, were too weak to do anything about this situation.

However, de Witt's preferred long-run solution for security on the side of the Southern Netherlands, ran counter to the ambitions of France. The original plan was for a system of cantons, on the Swiss analogy (hence, cantonment). If necessary there could be some kind of international guarantee, the nature of which was never clearly specified, to keep the whole area independent and, more important than that, also permanently weak. The idea of a 'buffer-state' between the Netherlands and their rapidly growing, commercially potent and far too powerful former ally was not a creation of the war that was later to come between the Dutch and the French. In the meanwhile, de Witt fostered friendly relations, as far as was possible, with the France of Louis XIV, whilst eschewing the

[1] S. T. Bindoff, *The Scheldt Question* (London, 1945), 109–37.

idea of a common frontier. As has been said earlier, Dutch policy in the first Stadholderless regime, long before the French attack was launched, favoured France as a friend, but did not want her as a neighbour.

During the Franco-Spanish war, which had gone on spasmodically, and with decreasing vigour, until 1659, it was still possible to direct Dutch dealings with France along such lines. The ultimate defeat of Spain in the Southern Netherlands was soon realized as inevitable; and de Witt early understood that the Republic would have to have some kind of hand in the ultimate settlement, which would keep the French as distant as possible from the southern frontier of the Republic. Moreover, as war with England for trade purposes became more and more likely in the early 1660s, some form of understanding with France would be clearly to Dutch advantage. The twin precepts of friendship with, though not proximity to, France could be accommodated, so that the United Provinces could get some French help against England without losing completely their buffer state to the south. This policy, so the Dutch hoped, was achieved in the treaty signed with France in 1662.

There remained, however, some outstanding difficulties. The major one concerned French interest in the question of the succession to the Spanish Habsburg possessions. Louis XIV was himself half a Habsburg. His wife was the elder surviving daughter by Philip IV's first marriage. There had been male issue by her father's second marriage, but the infant son had died in 1661; there were two remaining daughters and a further child expected, in the event the future Charles II of Spain. When the hoped-for son arrived, for a period the Spanish Succession Question, as we must call it, using capitals to accord it the status it assumed in European diplomacy, could for a time be said to have died down. But as the decade drew on, and the child was glimpsed around the Spanish court, with his exaggerated Habsburg jaw, his barely-disguised near-deformity, not to mention his obviously poor physique and his doubtful future potency, calculations began once more to be made. Other queries about the Spanish Succession were based on the fact that the French queen's renunciation of her Spanish inheritance, included in the Treaty of the Pyrenees, might be held to be invalid because her dowry, also provided for in the treaty, had never been paid.

There was also the argument about inheritance by 'devolution'.

After his second marriage Philip IV could be held only to have been a *usufructuary*, in other words to have had the enjoyment only of the wealth of those areas in the Southern Netherlands in which inheritance was governed by this custom. The actual owner would be his principal heiress by his first marriage, the queen of France; and on her father's death these territories would at once fall in to her and thus to her husband Louis XIV. Included among these areas was Brabant, richest of all and contiguous to the illogical Dutch frontier. French lawyers were commissioned to look deeply into the devolutionary inheritance laws of some of the more desirable of the Southern Netherlands provinces. They announced their verdict which was favourable to the French queen at about the same time as negotiations for the end of the second Anglo-Dutch war were getting under way. And Louis marched straight in to claim what he regarded as his wife's rightful inheritance.

When de Witt made his earlier treaty with Louis in 1662, it is unlikely that all these possibilities were present in his mind. But the Spanish Succession Question was already well in focus, especially in the interval between the death of the Infante Balthazar in the autumn of 1661, and the birth of the future Charles II in the spring of 1662. Philip IV lived only until 1665, and the plans for the so-called War of Devolution were being laid therefore whilst the Anglo-Dutch war was being fought. In this war the French did assist the Dutch, not altogether to Dutch satisfaction, as is the way with allies who are half-hearted and have other plans in mind. But they did enough to satisfy themselves that they had performed all that could reasonably be expected of them. There was already therefore some dissatisfaction between France and the Netherlands when France began her attacks in the areas to be claimed under her queen's devolutionary rights.

From the Dutch point of view this situation was exceedingly dangerous. De Witt's eyes were constantly over his shoulder as French armies came closer to the frontiers of the Republic, even before the Treaty of Breda was agreed. How could he turn what was only a 'snarling peace', as Temple termed it,[2] into something that would barricade his country from the approaching French, without giving away too much to the erstwhile English adversary in terms of his country's trade? Security against France might mean sacrifice of prosperity.

The withdrawal of French forces at the close of the campaigning

[2] *The Works of Sir William Temple*, I (4 vols., 1757), 311.

season of 1667 did little to reassure the Dutch. There was the feeling that France had simply retreated in order to come back in greater strength in the following spring. De Witt's solution was the 'mysterious', even 'complex' episode of the Triple Alliance between the Netherlands and England in the early weeks of 1668, 'Triple' only because of the addition to it, somewhat as an afterthought, of Sweden. 'Most historians,' writes H. H. Rowen, 'from that time to this have considered the Triple Alliance as de Witt's personal work'.[3] The Professor thinks Charles II had more to do with initiating this alliance than has hitherto been supposed. But in any case the treaty was in line with what de Witt hoped, and often feared, for the future of the Southern Netherlands, once Spain was no longer able to maintain her rule in the area. It would provide, so de Witt expected, a counterpoise to French aggression in an area in which both the two principal contracting powers to the Triple Alliance had considerable interests. It might at any rate give Louis pause for thought. Indeed, initially Louis's reactions to the alliance, though cold, were not markedly hostile. For he was given to understand that the Triple Alliance would assure to him control of some at least of the coveted Southern Netherlands areas. He even expressed a readiness to exchange for territories nearer to his own borders those provinces, to which he felt he had a claim, that lay close to the Dutch frontier. Moreover, whilst news of the terms of the alliance was filtering through, Louis was negotiating with the Emperor Leopold the first of the treaties partitioning the Spanish inheritance, should the Spanish Habsburg line later on come to lack male heirs. And by these negotiations he was expecting to obtain for himself very much the same Southern Netherlands territories as he understood that by the terms of the Triple Alliance it was proposed he should receive.

The trouble really started when news was leaked of the terms of the *secret* articles, especially the third, of the Triple Alliance. D'Estrades, French ambassador at The Hague, got wind of these through a spy in the office of the greffier, and simultaneously there came similar news from London. The spy at The Hague could not lay his hands on a copy, but retailed the gist of these articles; and d'Estrades reported to Paris that in the event of French demands exceeding what was laid down in the terms of the alliance, military action against France by the new allies had been envisaged. The

[3] H. H. Rowen, 'John de Witt and the Triple Alliance', *Journal of Modern History* (March 1954), 1–14. See his long list of citations at n. 1.

Triple Alliance has recently been described as 'a colossal setback' for Louis XIV, and this is how he regarded it.

Louis' anti-Dutch reaction was swift. Far from taking pause to think, Louis at once set about preparing a 'war of punishment' against the Republic, now regarded as an 'ungrateful' ex-ally.[4] De Witt attempted to mitigate Louis' wrath, assuring him that should Charles II of Spain die childless, the Republic would help France to possess all Spanish territories save those in the Southern Netherlands. But this Dutch attempt to play the benefactor was ill-received by Louis. So intense was his rage against the Republic, that he gave his minister Colbert permission to increase the high protective tariffs placed on Dutch imports into France in 1677. This is why the ensuing defensive war, fought by the Dutch against France for approximately the forty years forecast by Sir William Temple,[5] has often been regarded as a trade war, not a war for security. It became so later; but at first it was purely defensive. As we shall see, in the course of it the old principle, of keeping on friendly terms, but not sharing a common frontier, with France was replaced by the desire to obtain an actual defensive military barrier against France, with built-in guarantee by other powers.

To 'alert' the fears and suspicions of such a dangerous near neighbour as France was perhaps de Witt's greatest mistake. Undoubtedly in the four years intervening between 1668 and the French invasion of 1672, the grand pensionary's position became more and more difficult. This was to some extent the result of developments on the domestic front, as the young Prince of Orange grew to man's estate. Born in 1650, he became eighteen at the end of the year in which the Triple Alliance was signed. Naturally his gradual emergence on the Dutch political scene was watched with great interest by his uncles of England and Brandenburg. Louis XIV also was greatly involved. If William of Orange should come to power in the Republic, would he succeed in redefining his country's role in Europe, making of the Netherlands an active, even eager participant in European power-politics? If so, to whose advantage might Dutch resources be employed? These resources, we must remember, in terms of ships and above all of money, though not of man-power, still looked to be almost limitless, so the prize would be a great one. It was already foreseen that a Stadholderian Republic would be anti-French. It was likely also, with an earlier English

[4] *Journal of Modern History*, XVII, 14.
[5] Temple, *Works* I, 323–4.

alliance, and English influences around the young prince, that he would incline to the English side. De Witt's policy aims, of non-involvement, of putting trade first, would be hard to maintain if the House of Orange became once more powerful in the Republic.

De Witt gave much thought to, and took many pains over William's political education. The young man was made to realize the niceties of his family's role in the Republic, and it is due in some considerable measure to de Witt that even when his princely patrimony of Orange was taken from him by the French, William never cherished the ambitions towards sovereignty that had been displayed by his father and his grandfather. When sovereignty returned to him in 1689 it was independently of his position in the Republic. But memories of 1650 lingered on, especially of course in Amsterdam. And measures were taken which it was hoped would prevent the prince from ever becoming as powerful in the Netherlands as his ancestors had been.

We do not need to follow in detail the domestic history of the four years during which the Prince of Orange was emerging on the Dutch political scene. His final rise to power was the result of France's brutal attack in 1672. From then on William III was the most powerful in essentials of all the Stadholders. Under his guidance the Republic became a main retaining wall between Europe and French hegemony. And de Witt's political aims were perforce lost to sight.

Once the Forty Years War with France began, there was no question of the Republic being able to withdraw from Europe, or of being able to conduct her European relations with the interests of her trade to the fore. As in the earlier Eighty Years War with Spain there were intervals of semi-peace, when less active measures for defence were required, and alliances could be made with trade in mind. But the shock of invasion in 1672 was not to be shaken off lightly. It was long indeed before the Dutch forgot the spectacle of French troops held back from the western heartland only by the waterline and a series of what appeared to be miracles. From then on, throughout the eighteenth century, the bulk of the population still saw France as the major threat. And it was indeed invasion by France that brought the Republic to its final end.

The main allies against France came to be Austria and England. But before this situation could occur, big changes came about above all in England. For Louis's preparations for his 'war of punishment' included a treaty of alliance with England against the

Dutch. English opinion had been solidly behind the Dutch war of
1665–7. But once this war had ended, there began to develop that
dichotomy in England's foreign policy which is so marked a feature
of the latter half of Charles II's reign, and of that of his brother
James. There developed a split between the court and the country as
to what was to be England's policy in Europe. The Stuart-Bourbon
brothers were would-be absolutists, Francophile and respectively
near – and declared Catholics. Their court followed their lead;
some of the nobility were Catholic, and the children of James of
York, the heir-presumptive, were still quite young. Any palace
revolution, it was feared, would overset the tenuous arrangements
for their education in the Church of England. For James's relatives-
in-law, like him, had become ardent Romanists.

   On the other side the bulk of the gentry and the merchants were
anti-absolutist, Francophobe and anti-Catholic. But although
these were strong in the Commons, still the only source of adequate
war-finance, the control of foreign relations was still a royal
prerogative. Therefore the decision of Charles and his brother to
accept the initiative of Louis, and to support a 'war of punishment'
against the Dutch, was perfectly legal. The hatred of the English
royal brothers was directed not so much against the Republic as a
whole as against the anti-Stadholderian, anti-Orangist form that
the Republic's government had taken since 1650. They were
interested for various reasons in the welfare of their nephew of
Orange, and the Anglo-French treaty of 1670 promised not only
French subsidies to Charles II but also a chance to better William's
position, or so they thought. When we look at the terms in which the
treaty is concluded, we cannot fail to recognize a degree of animus
against the *form* of the Dutch republican government as well as
against the policy of de Witt. Charles and Louis were still
determined to 'humble the pride' of a mere gathering, devoid of
the personal attribute of sovereignty which both monarchs enjoyed.
They also intended to 'reduce the power of a nation which has so
often rendered itself odious by extreme ingratitude to its own
founders and the creators of its republic, and which even has the
insolence to aim at setting itself up as sovereign arbiter and judge of
all other potentates'.[6] The wounded feelings of Louis, already on
the way, perhaps, to megalomania, and those of the would-be

   [6] Quoted from Article 5 of the Secret Treaty of Dover, printed from J. Lingard,
History of England IX (ed. 1874), 251–4, and reprinted in *English Historical Documents*,
ed. A. Browning, 863–7.

absolutist ruler Charles II are here plain to see. It is ironic that the nephew whom his Stuart uncles thought unjustly treated, should presently dispossess James of his throne, as well as become the grand architect of opposition to Louis.

The 'secret' of the Dover Treaty, that Louis would help England's king to re-Catholicize his country, was not fully realized when Charles's Anglo-Dutch war, the third, broke out in 1672. When full realization came, there came also the knowledge that England's king had declared that he was 'convinced of the truth of the Catholic religion', and for this and other reasons, the Stuart Francophile pro-Catholic policy was rejected. By 1674 Anglo-Dutch peace was a reality, and by 1675 English troops in French service had been repatriated. But the Dutch were still under constant French pressure, and further than ever from security along their frontiers, or to peace in which trade could flourish and be furthered. Indeed, during the third Anglo-Dutch war and afterwards much carrying trade was diverted from Dutch to English ships. And after peace was made with France this trade did not all return to Netherlands channels. If the second Anglo-Dutch war does not mark a down-turn in the fortunes of the Republic, the third most certainly does.

The domestic events in the year of Dutch crisis, 1672, have been graphically told by Baxter.[7] Mounting hysteria, gathering crowds, murders, judicial or otherwise, brought William III to the fore, as much the saviour of his country from the French, as ever his ancestor had been their saviour from Spain. Like his ancestor, William had to fight hard. He had to re-create his country's army. He had to get it paid for by all seven provinces, those which were as well as those which were not in danger from attack by land. He had to agree quickly with Amsterdam, former adversary of his house, holder as ever of the purse-strings. He had to resist temptation to ally on personal, Orangist grounds with other rulers with grievances against France, including his uncle of Brandenburg-Prussia. His performace in these times of trial prove him to have been a very great patriot, a true Netherlander, no mere Orangist. But in no way could he withdraw his country from Europe. Under French attack he had to make, not avoid, alliances. He had to raise armies, diverting resources from the needs of trade. It was reaction to the French aggression that forced all this upon him. Dutch policy had indeed been changed, indeed been distorted, by the course of

[7] *William III* (1966), Ch. 7 *passim.*

European events.

Even so, at the close of the third Anglo-Dutch war, in 1674, and also later on in the same year, the Dutch did make some gains which later proved of value to their trade. The Treaty of Westminster, with its accompanying trade agreement of the same name also signed in that year, made peace between England and the Republic, and moreover safeguarded the position of the neutral power, at that time England, in any war in which either party should be engaged. The principle of 'free ships, free goods' was affirmed, and the definition of contraband of war so cut down that naval stores became permitted goods. Dutch historians tend to emphasize the advantage that this gave to England, which became neutral in the continuing Franco-Dutch war. It is less clear that English ships carried naval stores or other near-warlike materials to the French, than that French coast-wise trade was carried, in the war years, in neutral ships. It is true that once trade has been diverted from its usual channels, it is not so easily regained. Nevertheless, the Sound tables show that Dutch shipping returned pretty quickly to its predominant position in the Baltic as soon as the war was over, though England's share remained larger than it had been before.[8]

The advantages gained by the Dutch, in pressing for the inclusion of 'free ships, free goods' in the Treaty of Westminster, and in cutting back, as was their custom, the definition of contraband goods, were felt much more in eighteenth-century wars than at the time the treaty was made. For in eighteenth-century wars the Republic remained almost entirely neutral while England was at war with France. The 1674 treaty also gave the Republic, as well as English merchants when neutral the right to provide the enemy with naval stores, and to carry his coast-wise trade. From 1674 until 1678, English merchants enjoyed this privilege whilst the Republic was at war. But when England and France were at war in mid-eighteenth century, the boot was, we could say, very much on the other foot. There was even confusion as to whether the Treaty of Westminster could be interpreted to cover the carriage home in neutral ships of French colonial trade. By mid-eighteenth century

[8] R. Davis, *The Rise of the Shipping Industry* (1962), 224. Between 1668 and 1671 an average of 7 English and 158 Dutch ships entered the Baltic. Between 1675 and 1678 the figures were 128 English and 28 Dutch. From 1679 to 1682, 47 English and 179 Dutch. *cf. Debates of the House of Commons from the year 1667 to 1694* II, collected by the Hon. Anchitel Grey Esq. (1769), 348. Mention was made in debate of the 'sad effects' of the third Anglo-Dutch war, expenditure of England's 'blood and treasure, and *loss* of trade'.

this was a major source of her wealth. Moreover France was soon to become, was indeed by 1678 already in a small way a naval power; and her domestic sources of ship timbers were never sufficient. Fully exploited, the terms of the Westminster Treaty could have tipped the balance, of mid-eighteenth century Anglo-French wars, well over to the side of France.[9]

This was also true in a way of the Anglo-Dutch defensive treaty drawn up in 1678, when the Republic's war with France had been brought to a temporary halt by the Treaty of Nijmegen. This defensive alliance defined very exactly the aid each power was to render to the other, should either be attacked by a third. The *casus foederis* was limited to attacks in Europe, though later extended to preparation for attack. The treaty was part of the policy of William III, to embed the Republic in a system of alliances which would inhibit further attacks from the French. (Here William can be said to follow de Witt's policy line, taking much the same measures as his to safeguard Dutch security). But the limitation of this treaty's operation to attacks made or threatened upon either power's territory in Europe, did to some extent favour the Dutch. For by mid-eighteenth century Anglo-French hostilities were more likely to begin outside than within European boundaries.

The great patriotic Dutch historian Pieter Geyl thinks that the terms of the Treaty of Westminster, in particular, unduly favoured England at the expense of the Republic, and were in fact the fruit of complete Dutch absorption in the war with France.[10] Geyl relates how New York, once New Amsterdam, became by Dutch re-conquest New Orange during the third Anglo-Dutch war, but was returned to England, together with a substantial war-indemnity, when peace was made in 1674. He is, however, obliged to admit that 'in the matter of dealing with contraband at sea, regulations were even laid down that seemed to satisfy the old Dutch desire for a large measure of trading freedom in time of war'. He is also obliged to admit that the old *English* desires, to regulate Dutch fishing in English waters, to institute certain rights of search at sea, and to reach agreement on trade to the Far East, were not conceded by the Dutch. In other words, he could be said to be arguing that the third Anglo-Dutch war ended in a treaty which in spite of the French war

[9] Alice Carter, 'How to revise treaties without negotiating: Commonsense, mutual fears, and the Anglo-Dutch Trade Disputes of 1759' in *Studies in Diplomatic History*, eds. Ragnhild Hatton and M. S. Anderson (1970), 214–35.

[10] P. Geyl, *The Netherlands in the Seventeenth Century* II (1964), 146–7.

did consider the needs of Dutch trade. 'After three wars,' he states, 'the Republic was still able to maintain its position with regard to the other Sea power.'[11]

It is now becoming clear that although, after the French attack of 1672, the issue of security had to take first place in Dutch foreign policy, commercial considerations were still important. After the Peace of Nijmegen the Republic still thought of itself as a trading nation, not only as a country which was in mortal danger of another attack. But after the nightmare of invasion had come to pass, considerations of security had to take precedence over those of trade. The possible absorption of the Southern Netherlands by France posed a threat to trade, as well as to security. For Antwerp was still regarded as a probable danger to Northern Netherlands trade. And whereas under Spanish rule it was unlikely that the industrial areas of the Southern Netherlands could be revitalized, France seemed blessed with the initiative and energy, not to speak of the capital, needed to transform the whole area into a dangerous rival. On the other hand, were the Dutch themselves to expand, and to absorb even only a part of the Southern Netherlands into the Generality lands, would it still be possible to cut Antwerp off from the sea by tariff barriers? Antwerp was far better placed than Amsterdam to act as entrepôt for Northern Europe. De Witt had made this point in talks to d'Estrades long before the French attacked.[12]

Once the French had withdrawn from Dutch territory, Louis' 'war of punishment' changed its nature. It became instead a war to decide the ultimate fate of the Spanish Netherlands, though without much reference to their Spanish overlords. The matter at issue for the Dutch was quite simple. How was Dutch security not only from attack but from the economic advancement of her wealthier neighbour, to be achieved without any Dutch advance over the frontier?

The answer was a gradual change from the concept of a buffer state, *scheidingszone,* to that of an actual line of fortresses, to be garrisoned with Dutch troops, at first at strategic points within the Southern Netherlands, later on the frontiers between the Southern Netherlands and France. As its name implies, the Barrier policy was regarded as defensive, and it was never intended to involve actual conquest. The search for a 'barrier', which could guarantee the

[11] Geyl, *Netherlands* II, 147.
[12] Geyl, *Netherlands* II, 60.

Republic's immediate frontiers by inhibiting French incursion into the Southern Netherlands, began long before the series of so-called 'barrier' treaties. All students of late seventeenth-century European history are familiar with these treaties. Mastery of their contents demands mastery also of the geographical features of the Southern Netherlands. Their history has been told and retold and we are all aware of the international guarantee that the final settlement of 1715 achieved. Historians have been critical of the 'Maginot-line complex' that the Republic is supposed to have developed, once the barrier became a reality. But few have investigated its origins, or the reasons why such a policy seemed to the Dutch to promise a simple solution to the problem of rule in the Southern Netherlands. It is now time to retrace our steps and to consider the process by which the policy of remaining on friendly terms with France, but of not accepting her as a near neighbour, developed into that of a fortified line between France and the Southern Netherlands.

CHAPTER TWO

The Concept of a Military Barrier in the Southern Netherlands

Early Precedents   'The problem of the Dutch barrier', it is stated in the most thorough English treatment of the question 'dates from the Grand Alliance (September 1701).'[1] Dutch historians now take the genesis of the idea a long way back, even as far as the sixteenth century. For once the revolt of the Netherlands had begun, the whole of Spain's Low Countries territory had come to be regarded as a kind of safeguard at this time for the French against the ambitions of the Habsburg family. Moreover, this fire in the Netherlands, the result of spontaneous combustion in the house of sixteenth-century Spain, was blown upon by neighbouring England to distract that most dangerous enemy from attacks upon herself. When Elizabeth went finally in some degree of strength to help the Dutch rebels, she insisted on the surrender of cautionary

[1] R. Geikie and I. A. Montgomery, *The Dutch Barrier* (Cambridge, 1930), 3.

towns. Like the later barrier fortresses to the Dutch, these brought to her centres of influence together with facilities for trade. (Hence the reluctance of the States-General to part above all with Flushing to England.) In the present state of our knowledge it would be unrealistic to equate in any way the surrender of cautionary towns to an ally, with the evolving Dutch conception that the Southern Netherlands could best be defended from France by garrisons of Dutch troops in its strongholds. But the evolution of the idea that the Southern Netherlands would become a barrier between the Republic and France, ante-dates considerably the idea that Dutch defence depended on a line of military fortresses on the frontier between France and the Southern Netherlands themselves. This conception can be described as that of a buffer state with military defences at what appeared to be the area of most likely attack.

What then, was the genesis of the earlier *scheidingszone,* buffer-state, idea? A recent writer[2] on the topic has evidence that Johan de Sande, Professor at Franeker University, lawyer and historian, author of a contemporary history which became known under the title of 'the uprising Netherlands lion', thought thus as early as 1635. Dutch and Spaniards should unite, he wrote, in defence of the Southern Netherlands against the might and peril of France. Thus the South would inevitably become a 'division and separation' between the two countries. The buffer state idea is also, of course, expressed in the maxim that France should be sought as an ally, whether against Spain or against England, but that she would be objectionable as an immediate neighbour.

The initial move by the Republic to assist in the defence of the Southern Netherlands against France, was the Hispano-Dutch Treaty of 9 April 1668, part of de Witt's policy in view of the French threat implicit in the Devolution War of the previous year. From the Spanish side the lure was a large Dutch loan; but Dutch troops were also to garrison a number of towns in the Southern Netherlands. Two of these were to be in Northern Flanders and the rest along the line of the Maas; not only the idea of a barrier was forecast, but ideas as to the actual locations of some of the later fortresses can in fact be seen in embryo. Details were, however, not really worked out; and even the anti-French objective of the treaty was not underlined. Another Hispano-Dutch treaty, that of 30 August 1673, promised more Dutch aid to Spain, simply because of the

[2] R. de Schryver, 'Het eerste Staatse Barrière in de Zuidelijke Nederlanden, 1697–1701' *Bijdragen voor de Geschiedenis der Nederlanden* XVIII (1963–65), 65–90.

pressure on the Republic in wars with France and England. Still more Dutch troops were to garrison still more Southern Netherlands strong points, and in this treaty the anti-French objective was of course clearly more to the fore. In neither of these treaties was however the main Dutch interest as yet the creation of a line of fortresses which would protect both their own and their neighbour's territory from France. After the Peace of Nijmegen, which ended the first and perhaps the cruellest of the Franco-Dutch wars, Dutch troops remained, with those of Spain, in some of the fortresses in the Southern Netherlands, but still with no worked-out defensive anti-French plan in mind.

Very different, however, was the situation at the end of the Nine Years War. By 1697, William III had become King of England, and had led his two countries' armies in a long, expensive and exhausting series of campaigns in the Southern Netherlands. He had even laid siege (in Flanders mud) to some of the previously Dutch-fortified strong-points. By now the French were clearly seen as major enemies of European peace. The Grand Alliance, in all its shapes and forms, had been built up against the overgrown power. And William had established himself as Europe's champion. He had not, however, convinced all sections of his countrymen that all-out war was the only answer to possible French aggression. It is perhaps more accurate to see the emerging *Barrier* as a compromise, than to see it as the ideal of either party in Dutch policy. The reasons for this are buried deep in domestic tensions, between the Orangist, Stadholderian party, and the regents, or anti-Stadholderians, who stemming from de Witt were not by any means defeated in spite of the danger from France. To understand the nature of the Barrier policy, we must therefore return for a short while to the Dutch domestic scene. As we consider these domestic tensions, we must bear in mind that war is always expensive, and that the trading towns, above all Amsterdam, had to find the bulk of the costs.

The Crisis of 1672 The shock of 1672 inevitably increased for a time the power of the Orangist party in the Republic. William III was also extremely judicious in the use he made of anti-French feeling to further his standing. Geyl describes the domestic policy of the Stadholder during and after the French war as 'unattractive', and his actions as those of a 'violent party man'.[3] As was the Stadholder's duty at a time of crisis, William re-ordered the per-

[3] Geyl, *Netherlands* II, 150.

sonnel of town and provincial States' government.[4] He also greatly improved the position of the Stadholder in the three provinces which had submitted, some thought too tamely, to French occupation. For the remaining four provinces were at first in doubt whether to readmit their previous partners on the same terms of professed equality as before. Equality between the previously occupied provinces, of Utrecht, Gelderland and Overyssel, could not of course be a fact, because of the overwhelming financial superiority of Holland and, to a much less extent, of Zeeland. But the prince saw in this uncertainty a chance to improve his position in the provinces awaiting readmission to the Union. He offered them his protection and support, in return for their consent to a redraft of a document called the *Regeringsreglementen,* or *Government Regulations,* which laid down conditions for appointment to different offices. This redrafted document naturally gave more patronage and power to the Stadholder in each of the three provinces concerned. The House of Orange was also strong in Friesland and in Groningen, where the collateral branch of Nassau-Dietz provided Stadholders. Normally this branch opposed Orangist policy in the States-General; one of William's objectives was to keep his cousins as poor and as weak as possible. But if family feuds could be made up, Orangist power in the three re-admitted provinces, combined with the influence of the Nassau-Dietz branch in the north, might well adjust the balance in the States-General in favour of the Stadholder against Holland and Zeeland.

Geyl thinks that the combined effects of leaving the urban oligarchies in possession of local power, yet making individual members of them dependent on the prince's personal regard, were very unhealthy. 'Real opposition,' he declares, 'opposition of political intent as distinct from purely personal intrigue, was possible only for Amsterdam.'[5] Be this as it may, the prince's power just after the withdrawal of French troops from Dutch soil was strong. He had overmastering influence in three provinces, family associations with two more, and his position with regard to the Dutch Reformed Church and the universities was also con-

---

[4] On this, see D. J. Roorda, *Partij en Factie* (Groningen, 1961) who describes changes made by William III in the personnel of government in 12 of the voting towns of the Province of Holland. *cf.* Roorda's 'The Ruling Classes in Holland in the Seventeenth Century', in *Britain and the Netherlands* II, eds. J. S. Bromley and E. H. Kossmann (Groningen, 1964), 109–32.

[5] Geyl, *Netherlands* II, 150.

siderable. For the Catholicism of the French occupation, and the
reaction against this once their troops were gone, could not fail to
enhance the prince's power. 'Sound churchman' went with 'sound
princeman' as in days of yore.[6]

Having achieved the semblance of considerable strength at
home, William would have wished to turn with confidence to what
he regarded as his major task, preventing France from acquiring
the European hegemony on which he feared she was bent. But once
the French forces had withdrawn from the Netherlands, reaction
began to set in; and jealousy of Stadholderian power was as always
felt especially by the regents of Amsterdam and Rotterdam. The
allies of the Republic, especially the Spaniards, were neither particularly strong nor particularly co-operative. William's uncle of
Brandenburg, especially when he was attacked by the Swedes early
in 1675, made large demands for help which distracted attention
from the campaign in the Southern Netherlands. Together with
French raids from their captured fortress of Maastricht, this involved the Dutch in a war on two fronts. William naturally wanted
to build up the army and to keep it effective; but his domestic opponents, above all in Amsterdam, gave their memories of 1650 full
play. In order to increase his standing, not so much in the Republic
as in Europe, William tried to get himself sovereign rights as Duke
in the province of Gelderland. This created near-panic in Amsterdam, with a crash on the stock-market and a run on the Bank.
William suggested fortifications at Naarden, strong-point at the
northern end of the water line of 1672, near to the Vecht river and
not far from Muiden, traditionally the allegorical 'bit' controlling
the 'dangerous charger,' Amsterdam. Even de Witt had been unable to get Amsterdam to agree to such a step. Such a move from
William looked like the precursor of another coup d'état. Despite
this opposition, William was successful at least in getting his title of
Stadholder declared hereditary.

Above all perhaps William's English marriage seemed dangerous
to his opponents in the trading towns. This marriage took place in
1677. At the time, as her stepmother was pregnant and her uncle,
though married to a barren queen, still only in his forties, the
Princess Mary was not by any means a serious, even a likely, heiress
presumptive to the English throne. But the Duchess of York had
had numerous disappointments, Charles's queen was still very

[6] P. Geyl, *The Netherlands Divided: 1609–1648. (The Netherlands in the Seventeenth
Century I)*, 55

much alive, and James of York much in his brother's confidence. William III, like his father and grandfather, seemed to cherish dynastic ambitions. His father-in-law was a declared Catholic. Rumours circulated that William himself was secretly about to change his faith. All this, and the huge expense of war, convinced even William's most faithful supporter, the grand pensionary Fagel, that the time had come for peace.

The terms of the Treaty of Nyjmegen offered no sort of security to the Dutch on their southern frontier, against the French or any other power. As allies of Spain, and with the help of England, they had hoped to get effective garrisons in central fortresses across the Southern Netherlands. But only small contingents were permitted. Louis it is true retained only Franche Comté, Valenciennes, St Omer and Cambrai for himself. But the military position of the Dutch in the Southern Netherlands was not improved. They did, however, get some concessions, including the abolition of certain tariffs, placed on their French trade in 1667. And they regained and kept Maastricht. Otherwise the costly war, begun in 1672, ended in a Dutch defeat.

Moreover, it ended with antagonism especially between the Stadholder and the King of France. All the time circumstances were pushing William into playing against Louis the role of his ancestors against the Kings of Spain and yet there was within the Republic the feeling that a Stadholder could become too strong. The Comte d'Avaux, the French ambassador appointed to The Hague once peace was made, turned naturally to the trading towns, the source of opposition to the prince. Relations with the Nassau-Dietz branch of his house declining further, William had to face the French, the Amsterdammers and hostility in the two northern provinces. As Baxter puts it 'no one is less popular in a trading nation than an army man – when there is no fighting to do.'[7]

William continued to regard himself as the enemy of France; this view was also that of Louis XIV. The French removed from William his principality of Orange and prevented him from enjoying the revenues of his territories in Franche Comté. William endeavoured, but without success, to get Amsterdam to agree to the augmentation of the Dutch army, and presently made a direct attack on two Amsterdam personalities, the pensionary[8] Hop and Gerrit Hooft,

[7] *William III*, 177.
[8] Individual towns had their pensionaries, officials akin to general secretaries in function. The grand pensionary was the chief executive of the States of Holland.

members of the States of Holland. Hop and Hooft were accused of treason in correspondence with the French ambassador, but the prince was unable to press his case home. Naturally, however, this move threw fuel on the fires of Amsterdam's opposition to his policy. Finally, as an antidote to the prince's almost desperate efforts to reconstruct his anti-French alliance, Louis offered to the Dutch, as well as to the Habsburgs, a Treaty of Truce which guaranteed peace for twenty years. This was signed, against the prince's wish, by the Dutch at the end of June 1684.

The Twenty Years Truce looks like a staggering defeat for the prince of Orange. But circumstances were not anyhow then favourable for an alliance against France. Spain could hardly maintain her rule in the Southern Netherlands. England's royal catholic brothers were, it is true, temporarily apparently on top of domestic disorder, having defeated the Whig opposition in 1681 and used the Rye House Plot to rid themselves of opponents in 1683. But the emperor's troubles on his eastern borders were not over, whilst Sweden, Brunswick, Bavaria, Saxony and other German electors and princes had other distractions, and were unlikely to become bound together in strength, though the representatives of some or all of them were often in conference at The Hague.

Geyl thinks Louis himself precipitated the return to harmony in the Dutch Republic, by his policy towards his Protestant subjects. The revocation of the Edict of Nantes in 1685 is no longer regarded as a date of enormous significance in itself. But the accumulating effects of receiving so many Protestant French (and migration of persecuted minorities to the Netherlands was an important source of new skills, new capital, new manpower throughout the seventeenth century) must not be under-estimated. The accession to the English throne of the Dutch Stadholder's Catholic father-in-law in the same year as the Revocation, regarded clearly as a further threat to the Protestant religion, was also of some importance in restoring harmony in Dutch politics. French power had been increased by the 'réunions' policy. Even Strasburg had come in. What would be the fate of the Republic in face of an Anglo-French alliance? Was not the Stadholder, now emotionally anti-French incidentally, in view of the French denial of his (Orangist) unique claim to sovereignty, possibly right after all?

William gained one other great advantage in 1686, as a result of the better climate prevailing between him and his domestic opponents. This was the means to rebuild the Dutch navy, accomplished through a decision to farm some Dutch customs duties and to pay over the proceeds, a not inconsiderable sum, to the prince for this purpose. By 1688 therefore, the naval forces of the Republic were relatively strong. They were also under the command of the prince himself, for the Stadholder was admiral – as well as captain-general of the Dutch forces. Equally, although the Republic's land forces had not been augmented, the essential *cadres* from which they could be expanded had remained in existence under William's command. So that when at last the prince judged it time to go to England, ostensibly to pay what was not unlike the kind of official 'visit' a Stadholder would be invited to pay to a Netherlands town where there was a governmental deadlock, he could go with some show of force.

William's motives for his journey to England are clear. His own and his wife's place in the English succession had to be safeguarded from the claims of the infant prince born to Mary of Modena in June 1688 and universally regarded by non-Catholics as 'suppositious'. James might found a Catholic dynasty and moreover ally with the French king – a deadly prospect for the Dutch, reminding them of 1672. On the other hand he might be deposed and England become a Republic once more. These possibilities between them threatened both Dutch security and Dutch trade. Yet the anti-Stadholderians could only view with alarm the access of power to the House of Orange should the English crown go to William and his wife. We must surely agree with Geyl that their dilemma was acute;[9] and that by agreeing to further William's English adventure, they were cutting their own throats.[10] Not only was England larger and more populous than the Republic, and already in a fair way to rivalling the Dutch in overseas trade. Inevitably as an ally of the Republic she would receive, and retain, pride of place. And as King of England the Dutch Stadholder would put English interests before those of the Republic.[11]

The Need for a 'Real' Barrier. During the course of the Nine Years War, one of many that England and the Republic were to fight side by side against France, the concept of a Southern Netherlands Barrier of fortresses to protect the Dutch buffer-state took a clearer

[9] *Netherlands* II, 173.
[10] G. J. Renier, *William of Orange* (1932) 38–9
[11] Even Baxter, who so admires William III, has to admit that 'his divorce from Dutch life became ever more pronounced'. *William III*, 345.

and more definite form. This was partly the result of continuing
Spanish inability to mount any effective defence against ever-
stronger France. The Republic began to wish to garrison more
fortresses more completely than before; and much was learnt in the
course of campaigns about defensive possibilities in Flanders and
southwards. The fortresses finally agreed on ran from Nieuport on
the coast east to Namur. Additionally, some Dutch troops were
allowed in Luxemburg. Apart from the Luxemburg agreement the
arrangements were made separately between the Republic and
Spain.

These arrangements had the disadvantage of dissipating Dutch
armed strength, and involved the Republic in continuing expense.
But with the addition of some Spanish troops and some raised in
the Southern Netherlands, it looked as if the line of fortresses would
at least promise some kind of security for areas to the north of them,
near to the always hypersensitive actual Dutch frontiers. Moreover,
the presence of Dutch troops in Southern Netherlands fortresses
gave admirable opportunities for the advancement of trade. The
troops were to be supplied fron the Republic. Garrisons so
supplied, even more than armies on the march, require the
attention of their own service corps. Service corps can be furnished
with supplies surplus to requirements which may be disposed of
locally. This would be an easy way to set up in business especially in
a country like the Southern Netherlands at the end of the
seventeenth century, where administrative efficiency had run down
and become corrupt even by the standards of the time. The Barrier
of 1697 provided not only some measure of security from the side of
the Southern Netherlands, but acted also as a cover for Dutch
penetration into Southern Netherlands markets.[12]

[12] As did the final arrangements of 1715. See E. E. Hubert, *Les Garnisons de le Barrière
dans les Pays-Bas Autrichiens* (vol. ix of *Memoires Couronnés et Memoires des Savants
Etrangers* publiés par l'Academie Royale des Sciences, des Lettres et des Beaux-Arts
de Bruxelles, 1901–5) No. 4 esp. Ch. VIII and documents summarized at 8, nos 2 and
3 on 322.

CHAPTER THREE

The Republic in the War of the Spanish Succession

FEW if any responsible people in the Dutch Republic supposed it to be possible to opt out of the Spanish Succession War. The Stadholder-King had involved the Northern Netherlands as well as England in the partition treaties of 1698 and 1700, aimed at preventing either the Habsburg or the Bourbon candidate from inheriting the whole Spanish empire of Charles II. Such an aim accorded entirely with Dutch policy, since both security and trade were thereby safe-guarded. William and his adherents were moved mainly by the political danger of a French hegemony in Europe. The regents in the trading towns were already aware of French trade as their rival, particularly in the Mediterranean. Above all, they feared the establishment of French trade at Antwerp and elsewhere in the still potentially wealthy Southern Netherlands. When Louis decreed that French as well as Spanish but no other traders should have access to the South American 'main', he only increased these fears of France. Further, when Louis' invading armies turned Dutch garrisons out of the Southern Netherlands fortresses held under the terms of the treaty of 1698, the reaction was immediate. The Republic, already heavily loaded with debts incurred in fighting previous wars, would have to shoulder such burdens yet further.

The total Dutch indebtedness, incurred in fighting previous wars, is difficult to assess. It was held for the most part in the form of different provincial stocks, the largest being those of Holland. But there were other forms, town and generality in the main. The stockholders were principally Dutch subjects, and interest rates, therefore service charges, were not high. But even in his day Sir William Temple estimated Holland's debt alone at over sixty five million guilders.[1] A recent authority thinks this sum too small by half at least. The sums required for interest payments on these debts were raised from customs and excise; prices of all articles of

[1] 'Observations upon the United Provinces', *Works I* (1720), 70.

consumption were therefore increased, with inevitable increases in wages. Thus the process was begun by which, because of high and rising labour costs the Republic began to fall behind the rest of Europe in being able to export cheaply, especially from labour-intensive areas of production.[2] The burghers of the trading towns were well aware of the financial burdens they were carrying, and would have to carry increasingly in the future. They were totally opposed to undertaking yet further of these. But it had become impossible to avoid war, in the interests of national security. The Republic was obliged to fight; for France was no longer a possible friend and was therefore more dangerous still should she become a neighbour. 'The Republic', writes one Dutch historian, 'embarked on the Spanish Succession War without enthusiasm but with an exceptional unanimity of opinion.'[3]

As the war went on, it became clear that for the Dutch the primary grievance was having to work within the terms of the English alliance. The alliance treaty of 1678 had provided for mutual support should either power be attacked. Each was to supply to the other a specified number of troops and ships, whilst bringing all pressure to bear by every available means, short of hostilities, on the attacker. According to the then prevailing custom there was no limit set for the duration of the treaty's terms. This treaty had been reinforced when William became King of England, and in the Anglo-Dutch convention of 1703, on the insistence of the Amsterdammers, there was added to it a clause enlarging the *casus foederis* to include 'warlike preparations',[4] and thus assistance could be asked for even before an attack had taken place.

As the war went on, the English alliance became for the Dutch an ever more 'cruel necessity.' As was almost inevitable, John Churchill, later Duke of Marlborough, became allied commander in succession to the Stadholder-King. For although the Dutch army was and remained nearly twice as large as that of England, was well-trained, and well supplied with weapons, there was no general of outstanding stature. It was anyhow convenient that both armies should be under a single command. But the Dutch had the custom

---

[2] Charles Wilson, 'Taxation and the Decline of Empires, an Unfashionable Theme', in *Economic History and the Historian* (1969) esp. 118–25.

[3] A. J. Veenendaal, 'The War of the Spanish Succession in Europe' in *New Cambridge Modern History* VI, ed. J. S. Bromley, 415.

[4] R. M. Hatton, *Diplomatic Relations between Great Britain and the Dutch Republic 1714–1721* (1950), 96, n. 3, for detail about this important enlargement of the *casus foederis* of the Anglo-Dutch treaty of 1678.

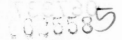

of sending so-called 'field-deputies', whose appointments were political, to preserve communications between their generals and the centre. In William's day, these people had been his men and unified command was thus possible. Things were different when the commander-in-chief was not a Dutchman. And Marlborough was unused to command by consultation.

We should not follow some non-Dutch historians of the older school, and over-blame the Dutch field-deputies for hampering Marlborough's plans for the campaigns of 1705 and 1706. But once the French were driven back from areas near the Dutch frontiers proper, Dutch policy favoured not an all-out war but a war of containment. A limited war, one with the defensive aim of not 'finding France on our necks every seven or eight years'[5] was the proper kind of war for the Dutch. The field-deputies were in fact pursuing their own national policy in trying to limit the war once Dutch frontiers were no longer immediately threatened. Such a war was difficult indeed to fight within the framework of the Grand Alliance. It was soon abundantly clear that the allied candidate for the Spanish throne, thus also ruler of the Southern Netherlands, was barely acceptable in Spain. The Habsburg Archduke Charles was a failure as Charles III. It was increasingly doubtful whether his Bourbon opponent could be thrown out of Spain, however much allied blood and treasure were to be poured into the war against France. And whatever the appearance of Dutch wealth, the Republic's resources were not inexhaustible. Amsterdam, which provided so much of the Republic's war finance, was raising loan after loan throughout the middle years of the Spanish Succession War. But she was finding it even more difficult to draw on her own citizens' resources, in view of expanding opportunities for investment elsewhere.[6] Low interest rates prevailing in the Netherlands made the task even harder; but the Republic, especially the province of Holland, and above all Amsterdam,[7] was

[5] J. G. Stork-Penning, 'The Ordeal of the States – Some Remarks on Dutch Politics during the War of the Spanish Succession', *Acta Historiae Neerlandica* II, 113. Everyone who wishes to understand Dutch foreign policy of the period should read this illuminating article.

[6] Rates of interest prevailing in England, where debt stocks were increasing, were twice as high as those in the Netherlands, and there were opportunities for capital gains.

[7] Between 1704 and 1707 Amsterdam floated new loans totalling approximately 6½ million guilders. Between 1707 and 1710 this sum was more than doubled; between 1711 and 1714 a further 20 million was added. Gemeente Archief Amsterdam, *Vroedschap Resolutien* vols. 47–49, entries under *Negotiatien* in index.

already carrying, and servicing, a heavy burden of debt. The offer of higher interest rates, which could have brought in more capital, was unlikely to be as popular with Amsterdam as cutting down the scale of the Republic's operations in the field.[8] And anyway although in some ways the Dutch were developers of deficit finance, they did not really like it. As the foundation of prosperity they preferred commodities and had a curious psychological attitude to paper as a credit basis. Even though as we have seen the merchant towns carried heavy debts, and with some success, the spectacle of enormous increases was terrifying.

If peace and security were the objectives of all sections of Dutch politics during the Spanish Succession War, how far were these achieved by the device, so well known yet so little understood from the Dutch view-point, of a line of Barrier fortresses? We have seen that the idea of a Southern Netherlands 'buffer', strengthened by Dutch garrisons alongside those of Spain in some strong points, had been evolving into the idea of straightforward military defence by Dutch troops alone, from 1697 until 1701. We are generally told that the formal arrangements made by the Austro-Dutch treaty of 1715, after the Southern Netherlands had been handed over to the Emperor Charles VI, were a great disappointment to the Dutch. From the English viewpoint, as well as from that of the emperor, who until 1713 was still the allied candidate for the throne of Spain, the so-called Townshend Barrier treaty of 1709 had given the Republic far too much in the Southern Netherlands. By the Townshend treaty a triple line of fortresses, to be garrisoned by the Dutch, who were also to nominate the governors, was to stretch across the area from east to west. Immediately north of the French frontier from Furnes to Namur the Dutch could garrison ten strong places, including Menin, Tournai and Charleroi.[9] All these towns had fortresses and commanded either river-confluences, roads through forests or waterways where banks could be destroyed to inundate the lines of march of opposing armies. They were also, it hardly needs to be said, important in local commerce or otherwise valuable centres of influence.

The next east-west line ran from Nieuport on the coast through Ghent to Dendermonde and turned south to Halle. There was no

---

[8] J. G. Stork-Penning, *Het grote werk: vredes onderhandelingen gedurende de Spaanse Successie-oorlog 1705–1710* (Groningen, 1953), 'Het doel van de Republiek was vrede' (The Dutch aim was peace) 453.

[9] See map below, p. 43.

question at this stage, as there was to be later, of fortifying the line of the Demer, thus interposing in strength between the Maas and the Scheldt. But Dendermonde was a place of great importance, as of course was Ghent, and Nieuport ranked second only to Ostend as a port of entry. The innermost line consisted of Damme, with access by canal to Bruges, and twin forts Perle and St Philippe, one on each side of the Scheldt below Antwerp. When the Townshend treaty was made, some of the designated fortresses were as yet unconquered from the French.

The *quid pro quo* of this treaty, which seemed to offer so much to the Republic – 'offered to them on a silver platter', as Dr Stork-Penning has it – was a reinforced guarantee by the Dutch of the English Protestant succession as determined by act of Parliament in 1701 and 1708. There was also to be a renewal of previous Anglo-Dutch treaties including that of the Grand Alliance of 1701, with its provisions about the recovery of all Southern Netherlands of Spain. It is worth remarking that besides the right (was it not also likely to become a duty?) to garrison the specified fortresses, the Republic could also in case of *attaque apparente,* station troops in any towns or fortified places in the Southern Netherlands where they might seem to be required. No wonder that Buys of Amsterdam, one of the wiser Dutch ministers, warned against undertaking too much.

When we consider Dutch 'disappointment' at not achieving the barrier as laid down by the Townshend treaty, we must also remember that this treaty was negotiated with that party in England of which the fate was entirely tied up in the continuation of the Protestant Succession. It was less of a party affair in the Republic. But the trading towns were not going to embark on expenses for a barrier in the Southern Netherlands unless it was going to be a viable barrier, as that of 1709 arguably was, and unless it was going to promise commercial advantages. The arrangements of 1709, from the Dutch angle, probably went too far and would have been enormously expensive. One can see why both Dutch parties agreed on them. But their aims were rather different, the successors of William III thinking in terms of security, their merchant opponents in terms of a real return on the investment they would be obliged to make militarily in Southern Netherlands defence.

From the time of the 1709 treaty's signature, big changes began to occur. The Whig party in England started to lose its grip. The allied aim of 'no peace without Spain' became more and more unlikely to be achieved. The expenses of Marlborough's

campaigns, and above all the terrible toll of life and of equipment at
the victory of Malplaquet induced a slowing down by the year 1711
in the allied war effort. It became clearer and clearer that to retain
any kind of European balance, there must be some partition of the
Spanish inheritance.

To achieve this became easier after the unexpected death of the
Emperor Joseph I in April 1711. Charles III, weak and ineffective as
King of Spain, became by October 1711 the powerful Emperor
Charles VI, possessed of military power ranking second only to that
of France. The Republic's Southern Netherlands barrier would
stretch across territory of a ruler who could, it was supposed,
protect his own. The Dutch did not feel so happy and secure as
might have been supposed, because the emperor realized soon that
he would draw little from the Southern Netherlands, and that they
could better be exchanged for Bavarian territories nearer home.
But even should Bavaria rule in the Southern Netherlands, a barrier
on the scale of the Townshend treaty would still not be required.
There were, it is true, Dutch efforts, in the year preceding the
signature of the final Barrier treaty, that of 1715, to survey the line
of the Demer, and to raise an *achter mur,* a 'backing-up' wall, of
fortresses between the Maas and the Scheldt.[10] It seems the Dutch
were more disappointed at being denied this scheme, than they
were angered at the failure to achieve the provisions of 1709. But
always the main objective was to acquire adequate guarantees for
adequate finance from the emperor. Without it the barrier would
become, quite simply, an embarrassment.[11]

The fortresses to be garrisoned by the Dutch, according to the
treaty of 1715, were eight in number only. They ran in a reasonably
dense line from Furnes near the coast eastward to Menin on the
River Lys. Tournai on the Scheldt might prove a hindrance to an
army which perhaps might choose this river route northward. But
Namur alone protected the line of the Sambre and the Maas, thus
the route by which the former French invasion of the Netherlands
had been deployed. There was also to be a garrison in
Dendermonde, alongside one provided by the emperor. And there
was to be no *achter mur* between the Maas and the Scheldt whilst
financial arrangements were to prove less adequate than they may
have appeared in 1715.

[10] A [lgemen] R [ijks] A [rchief] Fagel [papers] 1593 docs 10–13.
[11] *Ibid.,* doc 3. *cf.* A. Goslinga, *Slingelandt's Efforts towards European Peace* (The
Hague, 1915). 41–2, where national bankruptcy is shown to have occurred in 1715.

Stork-Penning sums up the results to the Dutch of participation in the Spanish Succession War in these terms:

the States had been drained of their strength and had lost ground to their rival (England) to no apparent purpose. It is undoubtedly true that the overshadowing of the Republic by England was inevitable in the long run ... but the useless prolongation of the war and the subsequent victimization of the States certainly hastened the process.[12]

Her whole assessment casts doubt on the accepted view, that the Republic pursued throughout the war a selfish, cringeing course, withdrawing from her obligations to her allies. On the contrary, the Republic is shown as more sinned against than sinning, and adopting quite rightly a policy that is best described as national, even pro-Dutch, in attempting at the early stages to limit, not to prolong the war. Dr Stork-Penning says in fact that from the viewpoint of the Dutch themselves the English presentation of the Republic's policy is 'hardly intelligible'.

Some time after 1759, William Bentinck van Rhoon, son of the Duke of Portland by his second marriage,[13] ardent supporter of the House of Orange, and of the Anglo-Dutch alliance, wrote an account of the Republic's foreign policy, in particular of participation in the Spanish Succession War which resembles rather closely the accounts usually found in non-Dutch historical writing on the same period, some of them still being perpetuated today. One has the same impression of weakness, of perfidy, of unwillingness to provide finance on an adequate scale, even of outright treachery in courting the favours of France, especially on the part of the regents of Amsterdam. Nowhere in Bentinck's account is there any recognition that these same regents were having to carry heavier and heavier debts in order to fight a war which was becoming less and less a war for objectives that were truly national. It is not very likely that Bentinck's account, written privately for the benefit of the greffier of his day, Hendrik Fagel the Elder,[14] became publicly known nor has it been much studied by historians of the Spanish Succession War. But it is significant that these were the views of a man whose correspondence and notes are

---

[12] 'Ordeal', *loc. cit.,* 140.

[13] To the niece of Sir William Temple. This lady was still exercising a profound influence over her son in the 1750s, carrying on the Anglo-Dutch (or should one say Anglo-Orangist?) traditions of her uncle's time, in a way perhaps confusing to the non-Dutch historian.

[14] A. R. A., Fagel, 1408a.

mainly in French, are widely known and have been extensively published. For this exemplifies the undoubted fact that historians who have left Dutch archives unexplored, whether for linguistic or other reasons, are apt to get a totally false view of the realities of Dutch politics at any period. The Orangist party in the Republic, especially after the days of the Stadholder-King, was much more international than the anti-Stadholderian regents in the trading towns, in the sense that they courted, whereas the regents eschewed, alliances of political import. The regents were of course interested in commercial agreements for the betterment of their trade, but like de Witt earlier, always tried to cut down commitments which were not strictly necessary in the interests of national security. After the Southern Netherlands had ceased to be ruled from Madrid, which promised no adequate defence against the French, and came into the hands of the emperor, defence by the Republic itself was no longer so vital an issue. The regents were thus pursuing a more national policy, in trying to cut down on the expenses of war, and to keep out of European alliances, than foreign powers who wanted Dutch adherence to alliance-systems gave them credit for. It is unfortunate in the cause of objective history that Bentinck van Rhoon was so prolific, that his writings are so easily accessible, and that his opinions have been generally accepted so uncritically.

There was a further complication, however, in implementing the ever-present, truly Dutch desire to couple security with considerations of trade in the Southern Netherlands. This was the problem of the English Protestant Succession. When the Dutch were first approached (in the early summer of 1706) about a treaty binding them to guarantee the arrangements made in the Act of Settlement, they were not impressed, for to underpin a domestic arrangement in a foreign country was unheard of.[15] But after the allied victory at Ramillies returned to the allies important territories in the Southern Netherlands, it became clear that Dutch policy should join their guarantee of the English Succession to an English guarantee of a satisfactory barrier. This 'peculiar reciprocal undertaking' remained the basis for the Anglo-Dutch treaty of 1706 and for the Townshend Treaty of 1709.

The peculiarity of these mutual guarantees consisted partly in

---

[15] Geikie and Montgomery, *Barrier* pp. 4, 44, 45. Note that these objections were raised first in the States of Holland, on the advice of the town of Amsterdam. Geikie uses no official Dutch sources, and does not seem to appreciate Dutch policy. See especially 46.

their becoming operative only on the Dutch side. The English Protestant Succession remained a matter of concern to the Dutch until a year before the outbreak of war between England and France in 1756. The possibility of a Jacobite *coup* succeeding against Protestant rule in England proved in fact to be more than nebulous. Nevertheless, in the years between the making of the Anglo-Dutch treaty in 1706, the accession of George I of Hanover to the English throne in 1714, and renewed attack by France on the Southern Netherlands in 1741, these possibilities could, and did, still frighten. A Stuart as King of England was a near-nightmare to the always-history-conscious Dutch, for they did not forget the days before their Stadholder William III removed from them the danger of encirclement by Catholic powers.

CHAPTER FOUR

Consequences of Aggression on Dutch Policy

BEFORE we follow the steps taken by the Dutch to help maintain the English Protestant Succession, we will consider the effects of combining concern for security with concern for trade, on policy towards eastern and north-eastern neighbours. The Dutch frontier in the direction of Germany was not completely defined even by mid-eighteenth century.[1] It traversed bog and marshland, especially towards the north, and there were no clearly defined natural features. From north to south no fewer than seven former imperial princelings shared some kind of common frontier with the Republic. The Count of East Friesland with his fortress of Emden, sat across the Dollart Gap. South of him was the Bishop of Munster, who had partially surrounded the Count of Bentheim, in his turn an intruder into Dutch territory, with an undefined border to the west. South of Munster were the duchies first of Cleves and then of Guelders, both disputed as to ownership in the seventeenth

[1] The Republic was also until 1728 titularly a fief of the imperial power! I. Schoffer, *A Short History of the Netherlands* (2nd edn., Amsterdam, 1973), 87.

century. There followed the Duchy of Julich, which pressed along the border of the Southern Netherlands and cut the Dutch off from their prized bridge-head at Maastricht. Close by were the territories of the Archbishop-Elector of Cologne, traditionally inclined towards a French alliance, who had supported and even maintained the French army which had invaded the Netherlands via the Maas in 1672.

It is clear that so diversified a collection of neighbours presented a problem, from the security angle, which differed from that to the south. From the south there threatened first Spain, and later France, both anxious to exploit the still great economic potential of the Southern Netherlands, hitherto the most industrialized area of Europe. But to the east there was at first a variety of territories, leaving room for diplomacy directed towards securing a balance of forces. The neighbouring princelings all had varied ambitions which could be put in the scales against their common anti-imperialism, unless they could with imperial co-operation achieve some limited objective against a more immediate rival. But as time went on there emerged in central Europe a great power, as potentially dangerous to Dutch security eastwards as France was from the south. The supermen of the House of Hohenzollern were not content to turn Brandenburg-Prussia into a mere eastern Germanic power. They reached also westward and within a century had claimed not only Cleves but a part of the Duchy of Guelderland, thus cutting the Republic off still more from the bridge-head at Maastricht. And in 1744 they also acquired East Friesland with its coveted fortress of Emden. Moreover, much Dutch capital had been invested by mid-eighteenth century in both Saxony and Silesia, areas coveted by Prussia in her eastern and southern expansion. The problems of security and of attending to trade interests in the east, came more and more to resemble those posed earlier in settling affairs in the Southern Netherlands. We will even see Prussia becoming part of a triple alliance with England and the Republic, fostered to guarantee Anglo-Dutch interests. The difficulties posed by Prussia's conquests of areas such as Silesia and Saxony in which Dutch capital had been invested also resemble superficially those in the south, where England remained the trade rival of her Dutch ally.

Dutch policy towards her north German neighbours was also conditioned by events in the Baltic. Here in the seventeenth, and for many decades in the eighteenth century, the Dutch fulfilled a vital role in carrying south the bulky Baltic products of ship-timbers and grain. It has been argued that this trade was of particular moment to the Dutch, because the bulk of the cargoes necessitated building large ships, with large holds, maintaining much warehouse space, a large skilled staff and other 'service' factors which could be utilized in other ways as well. But precisely because both naval stores and grain, not to mention metals, were of great importance to the European economy, it was also vital to western Europe that no Baltic power should monopolize the Sound.

Had the 1679 alliance of Lund between Denmark and Sweden remained in force, the anti-Dutch sentiments shared by these powers might have had serious results for the Republic and for Europe as a whole. But the alliance broke up very quickly, and the Dutch were able to achieve a commercial treaty with Sweden that from their point of view, and from that of their customers, was extremely successful. This treaty, that of The Hague in 1681, gave the Republic's merchants most-favoured-nation treatment, obliging the Swedes to disband certain of their privileged trading companies, and to drop attempts to exact increased tolls from ships entering Swedish ports. Shortly afterwards Louis XIV allied with Denmark, and was joined in this alliance by the Great Elector. As the Republic had become the ally of Sweden it was almost axiomatic that France should take the opposite side.

Brandenburg soon came over to the powers aligned against France, but the Baltic 'balance' remained undisturbed, which suited the Augsburg allies as well as it suited France. No warring western power wanted to involve the Northern powers in the coming struggle between France and the rest of western Europe. The Republic continued to supply both France and her own anti-French allies with the vital northern timbers and metals. They also developed yet further their own privateering arm, as did the English and the French.[2] Meanwhile during the Nine Years War Sweden enjoyed a period of prosperity[3] which came to an end only when Charles XII pressed home his insensate ambitions for eastern conquest. The allies succeeded in keeping the Northern, and their own Spanish Succession, War out of central Europe, which freed

[2] J. S. Bromley, 'The French Privateering War' in *Historical Essays 1600–1750*, eds. Bell and Ollard), (1963), 203–31, and a brief discussion in J. R. Jones, *Britain and Europe in the Seventeenth Century* (1966), 90–3.

[3] R. M. Hatton, 'Charles XII and the Great Northern War' in *New Cambridge Modern History* VI, 650–1.

the Republic from immediate anxiety about her frontier to the east, and kept German troops available to fight against France.[4]

When the Spanish Succession War, and the many various interests involved in it had been dealt with between 1713 and 1715, as in the Southern Netherlands the Republic was left with a compromise. There were some positive gains. In 1715 the States were granted possession of Stevensweert, Roermonde and Venlo. This gave them some kind of a defence of the line of the Maas between Maastricht itself and the eastern borders of the Generality lands southward of the main Rhine-Maas delta. But as upper Guelders went not to the Republic but to Prussia, the Dutch still had to suffer alien intervention between themselves and Maastricht. And they had to see demolished the two forts at Huy and Liége, which separated Namur to the south from Maastricht. This to some extent detracted from the considerable security represented by the possession of a garrison at Namur. The defortification of Bonn on the Rhine was promised to the Dutch by the treaty; but whereas the defences of Huy and Liége were destroyed, those of Bonn were barely touched.[5]

The rise of Prussia, the Republic's ambitious neighbour, at the beginning of the eighteenth century, was rendered the more dangerous for the States because of the Orangist connection. Frederick I, King of Prussia was the son not only of the great elector but of the daughter of Frederick Henry of Orange. Earlier Orangist family settlements had given reason to expect that if male heirs should die out, the female line might be advantaged. Therefore the will of William III, the Stadholder-King, leaving all to the Friesian cousin Jan Willem, was a blow to Frederick of Prussia. Worse was to follow, because when Jan Willem Friso was drowned in 1711 his widow became the sole guardian of the infant heir, later to become the Stadholder William IV; and Prussia's fairly considerable hopes of obtaining some Dutch eastern territory, or at least a few strong points, were disappointed. Perhaps we can say that William III saved the Netherlands not only from absorption into France in 1672 but also from Prussian ambition in the early eighteenth century for if some Dutch territory under Orangist overlordship had been acquired by Frederick I, he might well have pressed a claim to the office of Stadholder and the command of Dutch land and sea forces.

[4] *Ibid.*, 670. By the treaty's guarantee of Charles XII's territory within the empire.
[5] Geikie and Montgomery, *Barrier,* 357, 360.

As we have seen, Anglo-Netherlands relations had been closely regulated by a defensive alliance made in 1678. Any attack on territory of one contracting power, or on future acquisitions, obliged the other power to render armed assistance on a scale exactly laid down by the terms of the treaty. In 1703 when the Republic was under threat of French attack over her southern frontiers, the *casus foederis* of the treaty was extended to include what were called 'warlike preparations' in the diplomatic correspondence of the time. This enlargement of the *casus foederis* turned out to be one of those necessary crisis measures which later react against the country obliged by circumstances to take them in a hurry. For the defensive alliance of 1678 became, as it were, subsumed into the whole system of Anglo-Netherlands agreements, including the Grand Alliance of 1701 and above all in a Convention of June 1703, revived in 1716. But even by 1703 the Protestant Stuart line in England had failed, and the English Parliament had radically altered the succession, to cut off from the throne the Catholic issue of James II's second marriage. How far then were the Dutch likely to become involved in the defence against Jacobite attacks of the newly designated future Protestant successors? At first it was felt in the Netherlands that no foreign power ought to be called upon to guarantee a domestic arrangement of such a kind, even if attacked with the help of a common enemy.[6] But when the Townshend Treaty had come to be negotiated, as a necessary condition to maintain stability in Europe the continuance of Protestant rule in England was joined to the provision of a strong and adequate barrier for the Republic in the Southern Netherlands. The full title of the treaty of 1709 became the 'Treaty of Succession and Barrier' in the diplomatic parlance of the time. So the *casus foederis* of the 1678 treaty, extended to include 'warlike preparations' as well as all-out attack, could be used to cover the requisition of Dutch assistance for England, if the French should be merely rumoured to be assembling flat-bottomed boats in their Channel ports.

This could, and did, create serious problems for the Republic in the middle of the century. But at first the Dutch did a good deal more to protect the English Protestant Succession than they are generally given credit for. Their troops came over to England when requisitioned in the autumn of 1715.[7] They were transported quite

[6] Geikie and Montgomery, *Barrier*, 4.
[7] Goslinga, *Slingelandt*, 51–2.

rapidly to the North, and there gave a good account of themselves.
For the Dutch army at this time was still well-led and well-
disciplined, and the presence of Dutch troops in the North was of
importance because of the diversion of English troops to the west
country where it had been anticipated that the Jacobite attack
would develop in force. Dutch troops were once again
requisitioned, and again arrived, in 1719. Had Bishop Atterbury's
plot developed they would have been sent again in 1722, and were
indeed already prepared for embarkation in that year.

It will be remembered that all this time the Republic was under
the rule of the anti-Stadholderian party. It is interesting to note how
in domestic politics the regent oligarchs, especially in the main
trading towns were as always suspected by foreign diplomats of
being Francophile, and that the distinction made generally by
English representatives at The Hague between 'well-intentioned'
i.e. English-favouring, and French-favouring Dutch leaders was
accepted uncritically in the London of the day, as indeed it has been
since by historians. But under no circumstances could any Dutch
government ignore the domestic and public emotional appeal of a
danger to the English Protestant Succession, even if as time went on
it became less and less likely that the Hanoverians could be replaced
by Catholic Stuarts. There was a kind of 'finest hour' element about
the Republic's escape from Catholic encirclement at the close of the
seventeenth century. The Dutch had always long historical
memories. Their 'finest hours' had been mainly passed under
Orangist rule. And little by little the 'middling sort'[8] bourgeoisie in
the Netherlands were becoming convinced that only under the
Orangist house could they escape from their regent oligarchical
oppressors who were obviously becoming more and more corrupt.

In 1745, when Charles Edward Stuart, though virtually without
any French support, landed in Scotland to 'regain' his father's
throne, Dutch troops requisitioned by England were withdrawn
from the Southern Netherlands to join the English army which was
almost entirely repatriated. The French, with little or no cost to
themselves, had in fact won a major victory in the principal theatre
of the war. By this time the Dutch troops were not as well-led, nor as
well-disciplined, nor as serviceable by way of auxiliaries to the
English as their predecessors; corruption had entered into military
organization along with other departments of Dutch public life,

[8] This is probably the best, though not entirely satisfactory, description of the
growing section of town-dwellers who were not in regent circles.

and the troops were only barely re-equipped before embarking for England after active service in the Southern Netherlands. But at all events the Dutch government did carry out its treaty obligations, at a time when war was raging in the Southern Netherlands, the barrier fortresses had been overrun by the French with no difficulty at all, and when the Emperor was apparently barely able to hold his own against France.

Thereafter, the Republic, in spite of the return to Orangist rule which took place in 1747, refused to be drawn any more into supporting the English Protestant Succession in force. Twice in the Seven Years War there were rumours of troop-transports concentrating in French Channel ports. The first occasion was even before the outbreak of the war, the second in 1759; on both occasions the English ministers considered a formal requisition of the Dutch troops due according to the terms of the treaty of 1678.[9] But although in 1756 a request through the English representative was actually made it was never formally pressed, thus never actually rejected; and in 1759 although discussed it was not proceeded with. This change in the policies both of the Republic and England was not a result of weakness, indecision or pusillanimity on the part of the Dutch, as we are sometimes led to believe. It was because the Republic's ministers had begun to realize by then that their country's neutral services to belligerents were so considerable that neither England nor France would take any steps to antagonize the Republic so that she would join with either one against the other. If France were to march into the Southern Netherlands in force, an element of popular emotional historical memory would come into play and the Dutch government be forced into the English alliance. This was superficially all the more likely since the Republic was by then once more under Orangist rule, and acting for the minor hereditary Stadholder William V was his mother Princess Anna, daughter of George II. If on the other hand, England were to press too hard on Dutch trade with France, and as a highly privileged neutral the Republic was carrying on her erstwhile enemy's essential coastwise and Caribbean trade, then there was a danger that the Dutch might seek refuge in the arms of France. In either case the Dutch would lose much. But whichever she were to choose, if she chose at all, her ally could well lose more. For if joined by the Republic England would have yet more territory to protect, whilst

[9] On the earlier occasion transports were sent even before a requisition was made.
Alice Clare Carter, *The Dutch Republic in Europe in the Seven Years War* (1971), 61.

Dutch 'Barrier Towns' in the Southern Netherlands, 1701–1715.

After visiting the so-called 'Barrier' fortresses in which by the treaty of 1715 the Dutch were accorded the right to place garrisons, it seems clear that those in the west had different functions from those in the east that were nearer to the French frontier. Veurne (Furnes) lies on the canal from Nieuport to the River Yser, which at the junction with the canal runs from west to east before turning north to flow into the sea at Nieuport. Now a pleasant Flemish market town, Veurne had been fortified by Vauban early in the eighteenth century. These fortifications were destroyed by Joseph II when he came to the Austrian Netherlands early in the 1780s. From the high tower of Veurne's principal church the whole lower-lying Yser basin can be surveyed. Knokke, on the junction of the Yser with a now canalized tributary running from the watershed on which Ieper stands (Ypres, or to World War I veterans 'Wipers') was totally destroyed in the 1914–1918 war. Veurne and Knokke command points at which, given time, enough water could be sluiced on to the surrounding territory to produce 'Flanders mud' as in the First World War. The enemy would not, therefore, be able to get heavy equipment up to the defence line. Nor would he be able to take boats because by the judicious use of sluices the approach area would not be inundated. Time in which to prepare for such defensive, even semi-offensive use of water would be given because Ieper, always a market and government centre which dominated the area from the watershed between the Yser and the Lys, was very strongly fortified (parts of the wall, built in Vauban's style with enfilading fire-points, still remain).

Over the watershed lies Waasten (Warneton) where the Lys narrows to pass by the hill on which the town is built. Further down lies Menen (Menin) which crosses the river. Upstream there is now a sluice and on the Belgian side of the bridge to the east, i.e. down stream from the sluice there is a roughly diamond-shaped area of small streets three of which are named suggestively Vauban, Kanon and Arsenaal. There is also a fine late eighteenth-century building in the Grote Markt carrying the name of Joseph II and the date 1782.

Tournai (Doornik in Flemish) controls the waters of the upper Scheldt. The river enters through a gap in the rising ground on which the town is built, widens within the town and leaves it again through a medieval bridge, the Pont des Trous. Tournai's fortifications can still be seen to the east and south and are impressive.

Namur's citadel is built high above the confluence of the Maas and the slower-flowing Sambre. Behind the town to the north is a steep and still wooded hill down which eighteenth-century maps show only one road practicable for military traffic. The citadel is fortified at every turn and seems unassailable except possibly from the west, for the slope up to the western defences of the citadel is not so steep as to the north and east or from the River Maas.

Dendermonde, in which the Dutch could place garrison troops along with the Austrians, lies south and a little west of Antwerp. It is situated on one of the most important water confluences in the centre of the then Austrian Netherlands.

Thus the two western Barrier fortresses and Ieper had a different role to play from those which guarded the upper waters of the Lys and the Scheldt and the confluence of the Dender and the Scheldt at Dendermonde. Veurne and Knokke, with Ieper to back them up, could use water both as defence and as a battle-weapon, as the Dutch had done in 1672 and earlier. The role of the four eastern fortresses was more straight forwardly defensive.

Mr A. Bours, chairman of the Social Geography section of the Royal Dutch Geographical Association, a member of the staff of the Institute for Public Administration of the University of Amsterdam and a colleague at the inter-disciplinary Netherlands Institute for Advanced Studies in the Humanities and Social Sciences during 1973–1974, was so kind as to make possible this visit to the line of the Barrier fortresses and to accompany me. I am very much in his debt for the benefit of his opinion on the strategic role of the fortresses, and for many insights he opened for me into the nature of the areas visited.

Note: Where relevant or necessary both Flemish and French names have been given for the fortresses. Knokke and Dendermonde are more familiar in Flemish, Namur more familiar in French.

France in the same circumstances and in an area always regarded as dangerous to her security, would see an all-out English attack on her vital overseas trade.

In turning so early to the events of 1745 and of the Seven Years War we are perhaps looking ahead too soon. When we hark back to the Spanish Succession War and to the period immediately after, there is one aspect of Dutch obligations to protect the Protestant Succession which we must not overlook. This is the sordid question of cash. How were these troop contingents, due under treaty, to be paid? Even as early as 1712, when the question of England's debt to the Republic became the main issue between the two powers, England had had a sizeable public debt.[10] So of course had the Republic. Both countries were involved in raising the means to fight present wars from future revenues, because public like any other debts require guaranteed sources of some kind for the payment of interest. The Dutch had resorted to deficit finance long before the English were properly able to do so. It may be partly for this reason that the Dutch were on the whole temperamentally even less happy about this system than the English. In any case the hope of getting something back was naturally a support of that delicate matter, public credit, in other words a lure to attract further loans. In 1714 the Dutch rendered the English government a tri-partite account which in the end amounted to over £2½ million. The account was firstly for Dutch troops which had served in Ireland under the Stadholder-King, and had not yet been paid. Its second part was for expenses for mercenaries taken into Dutch pay when the Tory government withdrew English forces from the continent in 1712, and its third for sums of money advanced earlier in the war by the States to British troops serving in the Southern Netherlands. These not inconsiderable sums were only repaid in 1721, and in the meanwhile the likelihood, or not, of a settlement was used quite skilfully in the progress of negotiations directed towards attaching the Dutch to the so-called Quadruple Alliance, though the Republic never came formally into this arrangement.[11]

To these overdue accounts dating back to the days of the Stadholder-King, there were added even longer-standing English debts, dating back to the days of Charles II. These were finally agreed on only in the treaty of 1715, which Hatton thinks favoured the Dutch more than is generally realized because of the good impression made by prompt and effective Dutch assistance at the time of the '15. By the terms of this treaty, though the Dutch did not

[10] P. G. M. Dickson, *The Financial Revolution in England* (1967), Table I, 10.

[11] Hatton, *Diplomatic Relations*, 212, n.2. Hatton remarks on 21 (n. 1.) 'The correspondence, memoranda, and formal applications for the three debts fill a truly amazing amount of correspondence in the Public Record Office and the British Museum.'

get anything like the barrier provisions they hoped for, they did at least get an increased subsidy. The Dutch troops which came over in 1715 were paid and supported whilst in England by the Hanoverian government; and it seems that Dutch hopes of receiving a settlement of the 1712 account already described was one reason why their troops were sent so promptly to England in 1719. Townshend's settlement of outstanding Anglo-Dutch debts, on a Treasury basis and after subtracting from the total some monies due from the Republic to Scots regimental officers in Dutch service, and to Hanoverian troops which had helped to make up the 6,000 men sent from the Republic in 1715, for a time contributed to bettering Anglo-Dutch relations in the 1720s.

CHAPTER FIVE

The Republic in Europe in a Period of Comparative Stability

AFTER the Bourbon Duke of Anjou had been established as Philip V of Spain and his rival Charles had become the Habsburg Emperor Charles VI, the Republic looked forward once more to adopting the interests of her trade as the prime or even sole objective of her foreign policy. Her hopes of avoiding war were the stronger, because after the death of Louis XIV the French crown fell, by a process of dynastic accident, to the Sun King's infant great-grandson. The regent, the Duc d'Orleans, was cousin to the young king but was not the next in line to the French throne. The immediate heir apparent to the sickly child Louis XV was none other than Philip V of Spain. The regent knew that his cousin[1] had not been exactly sincere in his renunciation of the French succession. He knew that the European powers, above all England, would never allow a union of the French and Spanish crowns. He also knew, only too well, that France was in no state to fight yet another succession war, least of all her own. With some foresight, which was welcomed in England, in November 1716 Orleans

---

[1] Actually a first cousin once removed.

brought about an Anglo-French agreement. To this the Republic adhered in January 1717, becoming the third partner in the so-called Triple Alliance. This suited the Republic well, because the objective of this alliance was indeed the objective also of Dutch policy of stability in Europe. This was to be done by guaranteeing the Utrecht settlement, by maintaining the English Succession in the Protestant, Hanoverian, line, and by further ensuring the arrangements made for Dutch security on the southern, i.e. the French frontier of the now so-called Austrian Netherlands.

Thus in her immediate and still in popular regard, her most vulnerable neighbourhood the Republic had some kind of a guarantee for peace and security in her alliance with her English former companion in arms, and their mutual former adversary France. To north and east, however, the situation was not so satisfactory, although temporarily other interests than threats to Dutch security prevented any outbursts. But Prussia was now as near to the Republic, and in an area as vital to Dutch security, as Upper Guelderland. Prussia was now ruled by a king, and her ambitions were boundless. She was already possessed of Cleves, and was greatly interested in East Friesland. Hanover, and for Hanover the Republic's ministers had also after 1714 to read England, was desirous to expand towards the North Sea. The especial ambition of the king-elector was to secure from the Swedish empire, whenever it should disintegrate, the duchy of Bremen and the principality of Verden. Both of these lay along the line of the River Weser on Hanover's flank. Moreover the Baltic, so essential to the health of the Dutch economy by reason of its trade with western Europe, was still in a state of turmoil in the period after 1715 when the war-torn areas of western Europe were beginning to achieve stability.

For a time, however, the Republic was fortunate enough to see developing situations which did not require her intervention. She was thus enabled to embark once more wholeheartedly upon a foreign policy which could concentrate on trade. Prussia under her new king was indeed building up, but was not yet ready to deploy in aggression her inimitable military forces. England's Hanoverian king never succeeded in involving his new kingdom in the Great Northern War, in spite of Swedish support, with its considerable nuisance-value, for the Jacobite pretender. In 1719 the desired aims of the elector-king were achieved, and both Bremen and Verden were acquired for Hanover. Thenceforth the English king's electoral ambitions, though they did not cease to intrude on

English ministers' domestic policies, did cease for a time to divert English foreign policies into channels which might disturb western Europe's temporary equilibrium. Charles XII did indeed on his return from Turkey revitalize the Great Northern War. But after his death, with a disputed succession both to his crown and to his military command, the war was soon over. And when Peter the Great of Russia died, yet another disputed and imperfect succession turned inward the attentions of that other great Baltic power for almost a quarter of a century. The Republic also could now put domestic interests first; even though much pressure was put on her to form part of the so-called Quadruple Alliance of England, France and Austria, she never actually joined.

The 'Quadruple'[2] Alliance was designed to secure 'une tranquillitée solide'[3] in Europe, among its objectives being a Mediterranean settlement between Austria and Spain. The Republic was indeed here in a dilemma. Her financial difficulties were such that it was virtually impossible for her to contribute in any way to any show of force in the Mediterranean should such be required to achieve the objectives of the alliance. Moreover, the alliance was clearly anti-Spanish; and by joining it Dutch trade with Spain could be endangered. Further, should a Spanish war break out, to profit therefrom the Republic would, ideally, remain neutral. Indeed Hatton tells us that Dutch 'ships with all kinds of war-like provisions lay ready at the beginning of December (1718) at Amsterdam to proceed under convoy to Cadiz and Lisbon.'[4] Provided the 'war-like provisions' did not include actual weapons, excluded from the Anglo-Netherlands trade agreement of 1674, this treaty with its 'free ships, free goods' principle clearly stated, could be held to cover Netherlands trade as neutrals even with the declared enemy of their English ally.

In some ways it comes as somewhat of a surprise to discover that in the previous July the States of Holland had actually agreed that with certain safeguards[5] the Republic ought to accede to the 'Quadruple Alliance'. The Holland states reinforced their earlier decision, but only after long debate, in September, and more importantly themselves laid down the conditions. These were four

---

[2] We add inverted commas because without the Dutch this Anglo-Franco-Austrian pact was never in fact quadruple.

[3] Penfield Roberts, *The Quest for Security* (New York and London, 1947), 19.

[4] *Diplomatic Relations*, 184. See impressive list of sources at n.3.

[5] Hatton, *Diplomatic Relations*, 177, 181.

in number. The allies were to obtain satisfactory solutions to some of the difficulties still arising over the barrier fortresses, the Dutch contribution to the allied forces was to be reduced by half from what the Republic had pledged herself to supply to England under the treaty of 1678; there would be no obligation on the Republic to fight outside Europe and most important and significant of all, all parties to the 'Quadruple Alliance' were to guarantee complete freedom for trade and navigation in European waters. In January 1719 the States of Holland went even further and formally resolved in favour of adherence to the 'Quadruple Alliance', against the advice of the grand pensionary. But they demanded in addition a French guarantee of Dutch trade to the Baltic, and a promise that France would not attempt to profit therein from any interruption in the Swedish trade of Dutch merchants. As true representatives of a trading nation, the States of Holland demanded also, as the price of Dutch entry into the Anglo-Franco-Austrian alliance, equal shares in any advantages to be gained by any of the allies in future trade with Spain, or by England specifically in trade with Sweden when the Anglo-Swedish settlement should take place.[6] The States of Holland did not, however, carry their resolution to adhere, even on these highly advantageous terms, to the 'Quadruple Alliance', against the opposition of other provinces in the States-General.

It is generally supposed still that the Republic was virtually without any real political aim in failing to adhere to the 'Quadruple Alliance' of 1718. She is even supposed at this time to have been left, willy-nilly, outside the general European diplomatic scene. It is undeniable that some advantage in terms of status adheres to any country which presents a busy image on the diplomatic front. But to describe Dutch foreign policy even from 1713 as 'besluiteloos', a word used by Dutch historians and one we can translate as 'weak-kneed' or even as 'aimless' seems unjust. Immediate Dutch security was in no way by now at stake, since the possible war with Spain would be a Mediterranean one. The former violator of Dutch territory was a participant in the alliance, as was the new overlord of the Southern Netherlands. The general idea of the alliance was, it is true, one that was dear to the Republic, the overall peace of Europe. But the existing allies were well able, so long as they remained in alliance, to secure this valuable objective without the impoverished

---

[6] Hatton, *Diplomatic Relations,* 180–1, 186–7. It will be remembered that Charles XII had died on the last day of November 1718, so hopes of a settlement in the North were running high early in 1719.

Republic. There was no absolute certainty that the conditions for trade advantage laid down by the States of Holland as prerequisites for Dutch adherence would be forthcoming, even if the Republic were to come in. And as privileged neutrals Dutch merchants would expect to profit anyway from any war in which they could carry on trade on behalf of all the combatants.

The Republic's reasons for delaying adherence to the 'Quadruple Alliance' were thus entirely Dutch. First there was hope that Spain might come into a reasonable 'settlement of the South' (i.e. agree with her Habsburg adversary in Italy without Dutch intervention) and that the Anglo-Franco-Austrian alliance would be sufficient by itself to delay or to prevent hostilities. And even if a war did break out in the Mediterranean, the Republic's privileged position, as a neutral empowered by treaty to supply all but actual weapons of war to belligerents, would surely benefit her trade. The Republic's vastly increased debt-load, due to previous wars, in any case inclined her to keep out of war, or at least to limit, in as clear and definite a fashion as possible, any armed contribution she might be obliged to make to the allied force. The Dutch ministers dragged out the negotiations for their country's entry, by means of the Fabian tactics of which their constitution had gained them the mastery, until what the English dubbed 'the Dutch trick' made it virtually unnecessary to secure the adhesion of this fourth intended partner to the original alliance. For the disgrace of Spain's war-like minister Alberoni, coupled with events in the Baltic after Charles XII's death, caused continued war to seem less and less likely in the Mediterranean. It is true that the States-General twice, though without the strictly necessary unanimous vote of all seven provinces, agreed to send instructions to their representative in London to complete the space left vacant for a Dutch signature to the 'Quadruple Alliance' when the other powers' representatives had signed on 2 August 1718. The first occasion was early in 1719, but the Austrian representative took exception to the conditions which the Republic (really the all-powerful Province of Holland) had declared its intention of exacting before actually signing. In 1719, then, the allies can be said to have rejected the Republic as a partner. Indeed the secret clauses of the treaty, which might have involved the Republic much more deeply in hostilities than she wished or indeed was able to go, had never been officially communicated to her. Therefore, on the second occasion on which the Dutch representative in London was authorised to sign, this

only as late as December 1720, the matter was not proceeded with.
For the States of Holland had again laid down conditions for the
Republic's adherence which would bind them to supplying only
military, not naval, forces and only on a limited scale. There was
also a desire on the part of the Dutch to delay for as long as possible
the expiry of any ultimatum to Spain. The deputies of Amsterdam
to the Province of Holland also laid down conditions, accepted by
resolution of the States-General, which would as far as possible
favour Dutch trade with Spain, even if the Republic were obliged as
a member of the alliance to declare war. And they also laid down
conditions to safeguard their trade with Baltic powers. All these
objectives could in the event be better met by remaining outside the
'Quadruple Alliance'.

The Republic's partial withdrawal from the European
diplomatic scene after 1720, has tended to underline the impression
of weakness and confusion gained by all who read mainly non-
Dutch accounts of the period, or accounts based mainly on non-
Dutch sources. The views of Joachim Rendorp, whose memoirs
were written in the 1780s, may be accepted as representing the
attitudes to Europe of the powerful Holland province. Rendorp
believed that as the Republic was more dependent on trade than
other European countries, she was bound to avoid entanglement in
alliances, even in those which were purely defensive.[7] This view
reflects the de Wittian principles before considerations of security
began to overtake the need to keep trade to the fore in designing the
foreign policy of the Republic. J. W. Smit has put forward the view
that Dutch foreign policy was as 'intricate' as were the Republic's
political institutions, and he does not think that the time has yet
come 'for a full structural analysis of the historic trends' in the
foreign policy of the Republic as a whole.[8] He points out that there
was also an Orangist, more international, line, in which originally
purely defensive attitudes had been reversed. The Orangist
militarist, despotic, traditions were exemplified in the policies of
William II, by general agreement an unworthy descendant, and an
unworthy progenitor, of the great Dutch patriots William I and
William III. The heroes of the wars against Spain and against
France had at the time every reason to put their country's safety

[7] J. Rendorp, *Memorien* I (2 vols., Amsterdam, 1792), 33–8.
[8] J. W. Smit, 'The Netherlands and Europe in the Seventeenth and Eighteenth
Centuries' in *Britain and the Netherlands in Europe and Asia,* eds. J. S. Bromley and E.
H. Kossmann (1968), 15.

before all else. But by the period of the 'quest for security' in Europe, the Republic could with confidence retire from the power-scene to concentrate once more on the interests of her trade.

Critics of this withdrawal stress the opportunities for trade-*betterment* that the Republic eschewed when she did not come into the 'Quadruple Alliance'. In particular, a good deal is often made of the advantages Dutch trade to the Baltic might have gained if the Republic had sent convoys with fleets of both English and Dutch merchantmen during the Great Northern War. But Sound Toll figures do not show much deterioration of the Dutch position in the Baltic, vis-à-vis that of the English, until well on into the eighteenth century. Of course it is not possible to estimate advantages that might have accrued had Dutch policy been more forward than it was. But de Vries, who has gone very carefully into tax yields on cargoes of outgoing and home-coming ships, postulates merely a relative decline, not a qualitative nor a quantitative one, until well into the second half of the eighteenth century.[9] And Sound tables summarized by Price[10] show that whereas in 1681–90 Dutch ships averaged annually 47 per cent of those trading to Baltic ports, and English only 15 per cent, even as late as 1721–30 the Dutch average was still 42 per cent, the English 20 per cent. Considering how rapidly navies were growing during this period, an apparent transfer of 5 per cent from the Republic to England does not seem to reflect a *dramatic* change, although reasons are given by Price to show that the total of Dutch tonnage may have been falling faster than was the actual number of their ships. The Dutch actually sent *more* ships to the Baltic in the second half of the eighteenth century than had gone there even in the decade 1681–90, which in terms of shipping was the most flourishing, it seems, of the country's Golden Age.[11]

The other area in which it has been supposed that the Republic could have gained advantages had she become a member of the 'Quadruple Alliance' was the Southern Netherlands. Especially after the help given by the Dutch in the Jacobite attempts of 1715 and

[9] John de Vries, *Der economische achteruitgang der republiek in de achttiende eeuw* (Amsterdam 1959), Hoofdstuk II, *passim*. The author asserts that in terms of shipping the best years of the eighteenth century were better than the best years of the seventeenth century (*loc. cit. 2*8).

[10] 'Economic Activity' in *New Cambridge Modern History* VI, 871. See below p. 64.

[11] J. G. van Dillen, *Van Rijkdom en Regenten* with foreword by W. Zappey (The Hague, 1970), 339, 559.

1719, English diplomats did make some efforts to further certain of the Republic's aims in the Southern Netherlands. But it remains doubtful whether by the end of the second decade of the eighteenth century the Dutch were really prepared to risk more public money and more of their military strength in the kind of gambling investment represented by the trade of the Southern Netherlands. We have seen that some Dutch ministers were still hoping in 1715 for an inner line of barrier fortresses roughly along the course of the River Demer, between the Maas and the Scheldt. Engineers reported on this scheme in somewhat dubious tones and confined themselves entirely to defence possibilities. It is clear that to incorporate the economically significant town of Huy would have been far too expensive. It is difficult to escape the feeling that the trading towns came to regard the enlargement of the barrier as an expensive risk. And there was also the political danger of maintaining the needed extra military force, for army tradition tended to be Orangist. It is to be remembered that the Orange-Nassau Prince Jan Willem Hendrik Friso, Stadholder of the three northern provinces of Friesland, Groningen and Gelderland, was denied all chances of military education or experience whilst he was growing to manhood in Leeuwarden. This was to hamper him severely when he came to power in 1747.

The economic picture presented by the Southern Netherlands when transferred to Austria was anyway hardly encouraging. Pirenne's famous description of their fate under mid-seventeenth century Spain, 'le roi d'Espagne règne dans la Belgique, mais ne la gouverne plus'[12] applied still more at the time of the transfer. Lack of interest at the centre of government, hence long delays in getting answers to important despatches, and dependence, or the danger of it, on inadequate imported administrative personnel lurked still in the background when Vienna replaced Madrid as the seat of government. Prince Eugene of Savoy became the governor; but his interests were in the Mediterranean and in the intrigues around the emperor rather than in Brussels, and he was anyhow hardly a very energetic person. His lieutenant was an Italian career-diplomat who became the Marquis de Prié. Against his will de Prié did return to some of the Southern Netherlands provinces some of their ancient liberties, hence their local rights of control. But not all the provinces were lucky in this respect, and anyhow to revitalize the

[12] H. Pirenne, *Histoire de la Belgique* V (Bruxelles, 1920), 6.

economy of the Southern Netherlands required a great deal of vigour and experience, as well as much capital investment. For yet again, and on an even larger scale than before, the inhabitants of this cock-pit of Europe had suffered the miseries of being fought over by rival armies. This translates into demands for contributions from rival commanders, added to taxes to be collected by officials of the distant ruler, Spanish or Austrian. It includes the destruction, not once but over and over again, of installations such as cloth or water mills and harbour walls. It involves seeing seed-corn disappear into the bellies of hungry soldiers, and fodder stocks into those of their horses. Payments for such supplies to armies on the march, when made, are likely to take the form of paper promises, subject to variable degrees of depreciation. There cannot be much doubt but that the Southern Netherlands did not present an attractive investment opportunity to private Dutch capital in the period following the War of the Spanish Succession,[13] even if we do not take into account the increasing trend towards 'aristocratization' in Dutch society. This was tending anyway to encourage wealthy Dutchmen to place their capital in non-Dutch enterprises or public debts which promised high and steady yields and appreciation. Risky improvement schemes in the Southern Netherlands were not likely to attract the investment surpluses of people such as these.

The Dutch government, also, was dubious about further commitment in the Southern Netherlands, especially when it became clear how badly damaged were the fortifications of the places allotted to the Republic by the Barrier Treaty of 1715. Without a good deal of Austrian money, as Amsterdam declared, accessions to these would prove 'embarrassing'. The finances of the emperor were well-known to be in a serious state. The Dutch ministers were naturally anxious to make sure that any imperial promises would be honoured. But how to be certain? Even had they

---

[13] It is true that first Spanish silver from the Main, and later Austrian silver from Imperial mines in central and eastern Europe, found its way northward to the Republic. But this was the result of Dutch trade with the Southern Netherlands' conquerors. It was in no way an incentive to Dutch enterprise directed towards rehabilitating the trade of the area or of its inhabitants. I owe this information to Professor van Houtte, of Louvain University. In general on the Austrian Netherlands see J. W. Stoye, 'The Austrian Habsburgs' in *New Cambridge Modern History* VI, 598, N. Laude *La Compagnie d'Ostende et son activité coloniale au Bengale 1725–1730* (Bruxelles, 1944), 10, and M. Huisman, *La Belgique Commerciale sous l'Empereur Charles VI.* (Bruxelles et Paris, 1902).

gone whole-heartedly into the 'Quadruple Alliance', they could not be certain that the imperial contributions would be forthcoming both regularly and in full. But the major Dutch concern was over trade to the Indies from Ostend. The fact that this trade was well under way before the foundation of the famous Ostend East India Company with some measure of imperial backing, is often overlooked. No fewer than twelve ships plied between Ostend and the Bengal coast in 1720, and this trade had been going on since 1714. Many of the captains and, significantly, many of the owners of these vessels were English or Scots,[14] and one at least was an Amsterdammer. The profits could be enormous, 56 per cent on investment had been rumoured in one case. But it was soon found that competition among individual ships' captains, and secrecy as to goods taken to Indian markets, or brought home from thence, could result in losses all round. So early in 1723 the Imperial and Royal Company for trade with the Indies was founded, to impose a little order and regulation in this trade which had been going on fairly regularly since 1714, mainly from Ostend. Says one of its historians 'la Compagnie Imperiale des Indes établie dans les Pays-Bas n'a pas été créé brusquement de rien,'[15]

It was not however until the company looked like becoming a fairly paying proposition that the English and the Dutch took fright. Both countries knew that good organization could bring big profits by trade to the Far East, and therefore both England and the Republic united to use for the destruction of the Company the element of doubt which arose as to the succession to Charles VI. It is well known that the Dutch as well as the English guarantee of the document, known superficially to non-Austrian historians as the 'Pragmatic Sanction', was gained by the suppression of the Ostend East India Company. This is too simple an explanation, and leaves out of account any idea as to the Company's scale of operations and of its effect on the economy of the Southern Netherlands. It seems that after incorporation the Company did prosper for a time (Huisman heads one chapter of his book 'L'âge d'or de la Compagnie d'Ostende',[16] this for a short time after 1725). But there was constant danger from Algerian pirates, a need therefore to equip convoy vessels. And although the China ventures brought

---

[14] Who were interested in supplying the rapidly-expanding market for tea in England and Scotland.

[15] Laude, *Compagnie d'Ostende*, 24.

[16] *Op. cit.* 355ff.

back high dividends, those to the coast of Bengal, where factories
with expensive defence needs had to be established, were apt to be
losers. Huisman blames England for encouraging the Algerian
pirates to pursue Ostend East India Company's ships even as far
north as the Channel, and thinks that English and Dutch agents
spread discouraging rumours about the Company's affairs,
whereby 'une panique se déclara' and stockprices fell sharply owing
to panic sales, including the stock of Prince Eugene of Savoy, who
held sixty shares.

There were between 150 and 200 shareholders in the Ostend East
India Company. Expatriate English and Irish Jacobites, that is to
say mainly catholics, were influential in its development and it is
possible that some shareholders were among them. It is not likely
that much, if any, Dutch money was invested in this Company, for it
soon became recognized as a dangerous rival to those of the
Netherlands and England in which Dutch merchants had money
invested. It was beginning to look as if the European market for Far
Eastern products was becoming selective. Huisman remarks sadly
of the returning cargoes of 1726 in Ostend East Indiamen, 'par
suite de l'abondance des produits asiatiques qui encombraient les
marchés d'Amsterdam et de Londres, la vente ne donna pas les
résultats esperés.'[17] In an age when internationalism had not yet
evolved to the stage in which economic organization, in the interests
of price-maintenance, became possible, it seems scarcely fair to
blame the Dutch for directing their policy towards putting down a
dangerous rival.

For this is what they did. With their Baltic trade in no danger, and
like that to the Mediterranean, profiting most from their remaining
neutral, the Dutch were able for a few years to stand on one side
whilst the other powers were busy extending some of their own
interests at some of their rivals' expense; this was all within the
framework of maintaining peace in Europe, a situation of course
favourable to the Republic's interests. But towards the middle of
the 1720s the situation began to look rather different. This was
because the Ostend East India Company began to show signs of
becoming a serious rival to that of the Republic – it will be
remembered that its Golden Age has been dated from around 1725.
Also, there were two important succession issues hanging over
Europe, one that to Charles VI, the other that to the duchies of

---

[17] *Belgique Commerciale*, 362.

Jülich and Berg,[18] right on the Republic's eastern frontier. The
succession to Jülich and Berg was greatly coveted by Frederick, King
of Prussia, who also had an interest in eastern Dutch territory
proper, due to his being the son of an Orangist princess, as well as
of the Great Elector. Frederick of Prussia had already laid claim to
some Dutch territories, had even erected toll barriers on the Maas
and made other attempts at exacting sums of money from Dutch
traders in the regions where he claimed illusory rights.[19]

By the mid-seventeen-twenties Europe was aligned in two
initially overtly non-hostile but all the same threatening camps. The
Vienna powers, Austria and Spain, made some attempt to achieve a
Dutch alliance, but the Republic stood out. For good Dutch
reasons, however, the Republic joined the rival Alliance of
Hanover, formed in 1725 between England, France and Prussia;
but she did not join at once; and she joined on terms which
favoured her rather than the allies. First of all, the formation of the
Hanover Alliance (so-called because the opposition in the English
Parliament decided that it favoured Hanoverian interests) naturally
strengthened the bond between the powers of the Vienna treaty,
and thus sent those of Hanover seeking for further adherents.
Although England had not hitherto reacted very strongly against
the Ostend East India Company,[20] she showed her readiness to
oblige the Dutch by declaring for their trade rival's suppression, if
they would come into the alliance. The Hanover powers did at first
take pains to conceal from the Dutch the Prussian-favouring
attitude they were preparing to adopt towards the Jülich-Berg
succession issue.[21] But they were ready to meet Dutch objections to
guaranteeing in general the Westphalia and Oliva treaties (the latter
of particular moment to the King of Prussia) which they had agreed
on themselves but to which the Republic, always fearful of
seemingly unnecessary commitment, was not prepared to accede.
But in the almost ten months' interval before the Republic came
into the alliance, the attitude of Prussia underwent a change.
Frederick William began to wonder whether he might not do better

[18] A. M. Wilson, *French Foreign Policy during the Administration of Cardinal Fleury
1726–1743*, Harvard Historical Studies XL, 153–4. 'To secure support for this claim
(to the succession) became as important an aim to the King of Prussia as to secure
recognition for the Pragmatic Sanction was to the Emperor' writes Wilson.

[19] Goslinga, *Slingelandt*, 93.

[20] Goslinga, *Slingelandt*, 90–1.

[21] By the fourth separate article, by which France and Great Britain agreed to
support the 'just claims' of Prussia. Wilson, *Foreign Policy*, 154–5.

by adhering to the emperor, than remaining in an alliance which seemed to be becoming more and more anti-imperial. Moreover during 1726 both the pro-Austrian Spanish minister Ripperda, and the Spanish-offending French minister the Duc de Bourbon were replaced. New alliances became possible and the new French minister, Cardinal Fleury, saw the necessity of maintaining peace in Europe, if only to prevent the outbreak of yet another full-scale succession war centring this time on the Empire. The belated Dutch adherence to the Alliance of Hanover brought the Republic prospects of peace in Europe, England's support over the suppression of the Ostend East India Company and no obligation to prior agreement to any previous European settlements. This was enough to be going on with, for the Jülich-Berg succession issue was not yet by any means at crisis point.

The Republic thus became aligned with the powers in whose interest European peace loomed large. Its delegates attended the congress of Soissons, to which the Dutch pensionary Slingelandt presented a memorial suggesting that the representatives of so many powers assembled there together should attempt to settle the major questions that contemporarily seemed to threaten the peace of Europe.

Slingelandt's memorial, which he called 'Pensées Impartiales et Pacifiques'[22] advocated the settlement, without recourse to any war, of the succession to Charles VI. For Europe could not contemplate another succession war on the scale of that which had taken place over the inheritance to the Spanish Habsburg dominions after the death of Charles II. He thought that the powers should give the guarantee desired by the emperor, who would be prepared to render some kind of *quid pro quo* to the Hanover allies. This memorial forms, according to Wilson, the principal claim of Slingelandt to have made 'efforts towards European peace';[23] but the matter could not of course be solved by a straight-forward agreement among the Hanover allies that Maria Theresa should succeed to her father's possessions. Dynastic interests of the Queen of Spain threatened war in Italy, and divided the Vienna powers. France was not at all eager to guarantee the Pragmatic Sanction. Prussia, now veering even farther towards the emperor, was a threat to the peaceful settlement of Europe's affairs by reason of her

[22] Goslinga, *Slingelandt*, 371.
[23] Wilson, *Foreign Policy*, 192.

military strength. She was also interfering in the affairs of East Friesland. Hanoverian considerations complicated England's European attitudes; and questions about the Southern Netherlands complicated those of the Republic. In the end, the Republic came quite well out of the confused and difficult discussions at Soissons. She acceded without delay to the Anglo-Franco-Spanish Treaty of Seville, which as Goslinga has it turned the Triple Alliance of Hanover into a Quadruple Alliance of England, France, Spain and the Republic.[24] This treaty brought the Dutch trading advantages in the Mediterranean, for Spain agreed to return to earlier treaty terms with the Republic which had favoured her merchants at the expense of those of other nationals. It obliged the Dutch to send only half as many troops (as the other powers) should an Austro-Spanish war break out in Italy. It obtained them most-favoured-nation treatment as regards the subjects and allies of Spain, (and for what it was worth it got them from Spain the coveted title 'Hauts et Puissants Seigneurs'). France as well as England agreed to help put down the Ostend East India Company, and agreed to regulate in the Dutch rather than in the Prussian sense the troubled affairs of East Friesland. Should the Republic suffer any attack, the Seville powers agreed to come to her rescue on a larger scale than she was herself obliged to in the case of attacks on her allies. Admittedly, the Republic was more fortunate than forceful in achieving these desirable aims, because her association with the other Seville powers was a matter of moment to them. But her policy in taking hold of opportunities, and making the utmost of them, can hardly be fairly described as 'besluiteloos', inconclusive or weak-kneed.

The same is surely true of Dutch reactions when the Polish 'succession' threatened yet another war to decide who should sit upon a throne. We need not yet again recount the details of this affair. But we should note that, well before the French declared war on the emperor, they had approached the Dutch to find out whether if France agreed not to carry the war into the Austrian Netherlands, the Republic would declare itself neutral. Of course the Dutch ministers agreed to so favourable an arrangement. The Convention of Neutrality was signed at the end of 1733, incidentally without any consultation with the British.[25] For contrary to generally-held opinion, the prolonged negotiations for a marriage between the Prince of Orange-Nassau and the English Princess

[24] Goslinga, *Slingelandt*, 388.   [25] Wilson, *Foreign Policy*, 245–6.

Royal were not regarded in the Netherlands as marking a closer Anglo-Dutch alliance. A war in central Germany, provided it did not erupt into the Southern Netherlands, was from the Dutch point of view an advantage, for it was virtually certain that such a war would spread to the Mediterranean and thus advantage Netherlands neutral trade. The English ministers were not by any means ignorant of the French proposals, or of the likely Dutch reaction, but according to Wilson 'they simply were unable to think of any means to prevent' the Franco-Dutch convention of neutrality.[26] Once the Dutch had declared themselves neutral, the British government followed. The Dutch action can thus be regarded as an important step towards limiting the area of the war. As a result of remaining neutral, both countries' trade benefited. But it is likely that trade of the other neutral power, Great Britain, benefited more than that of the Netherlands. For as we shall see, the Republic was at this time already beginning to suffer considerably from the combined effects of relative economic decline and of natural disaster.

Both neutral powers, Great Britain and the Republic, attempted to mediate in the war, offering 'good offices' to France as early as February 1734. These were at first accepted, but without any serious intention; and peace was made between France and the emperor without any serious intervention by the Maritime Powers. In the 1730s the initiative in European power-alignment was with France rather than with Great Britain, still less with the Republic. This suited both, since their subjects could continue to concentrate, the one on overseas concerns, the other on trade with the Baltic, the Mediterranean and the Far East. But the temporary absence of both Maritime Powers from the European diplomatic front must still not be regarded as marking any increase in friendly relations between them. For rivalry could not fail to grow out of such concentration on trade. And the link which we must soon examine between the houses of Hanover and Orange, at a time when the Republic was without a Stadholder, was also provocative of Anglo-Netherlands tension. It is now necessary to survey the domestic scene in the Republic and to assess the effects of its tensions on her policy as a European power.

[26] *Ibid., Foreign Policy*, 246, n. 17. The source is a letter from the Duke of Newcastle to Sir Thomas Robinson.

CHAPTER SIX

The Domestic Problems of the United Provinces and the Motivation of Dutch Neutrality in the Second Stadholderless Regime, 1702–1747

DR Stork-Penning, in the introductory paragraphs of the *Acta* article referred to previously, has some interesting reflections on why so black a picture has been painted of Dutch politics and policies in the eighteenth century, but her judgment might well also apply to what has been written about the Republic in the period between 1715 and 1740; for always in foreign accounts shortcomings are enlarged upon, whilst difficulties are overlooked or discounted. The difficulties in the Dutch domestic situation, which we now have to take into account, lay in the fields of government, of leadership, of social change, of gradual economic run-down, but above all in the field of central government finance. The true picture has been distorted because non-Dutch historians have relied too much on what was written home by foreign representatives at The Hague, and by alien residents and visitors, and not very much effort has been made to tackle Dutch records or to use those works of modern Dutch historians which are record-based. The Dutch record material of the eighteenth century is indeed not easy to use. There is a great deal of it, and it is dispersed all over the Netherlands by reason of the continuing element of provincial autonomy. Nearly all the big cities have their own repositories which often contain material of far more than local interest. And by the eighteenth century there was an even greater tendency than previously for ministers to demand copies of all important documents, to take extracts from these for their own information, but to refrain from indicating clearly where the unextracted passages occur in the original. There are thus many pitfalls; and the novice is apt to be overcome and to retreat thankfully to the Public Record Office in London, or to the Paris Foreign Office archives where he can obtain and read easily a clearly defined series of letters which appear to explain lucidly and knowledgeably what was going on at any time in the Republic.

The trouble with these foreigners' accounts is that no foreign statesman or representative was ever really successful in manipulating Dutch policy to suit his superior. There was thus even a career-motive in exaggerating the indecisiveness or aimlessness of Dutch policy-makers. The fact that the best, one might say even the only possible policy for the Republic was to remain lightly committed was thus obscured beneath the necessity to magnify governmental failings and weakness in leadership, whilst minimizing the various catastrophes which added to Dutch governmental difficulties.

In the field of government, there were first of all the difficulties of decentralization. We do not need to elaborate here what has been said on this subject in the Introduction. But it must once more be emphasized that the most powerful province, that of Holland, with its most powerful component, Amsterdam, was most deeply committed to maintaining stable conditions for trade, whilst being least at risk when questions of security became prominent. It was also, because of the history of bad relations between Amsterdam and the House of Orange, and because of the high proportion of any costs both Amsterdam and the province of Holland had to carry, the least inclined to put money into measures for defence. This was not, as *English* representatives united in averring, because either province or city was governed by people who were pro-French. It was simply that the policy advocated by this powerful section of the Republic was one of non-alignment and measures to promote trade. Equally, as the *French* representatives united in averring, the provinces with frontiers bordering on central Europe were not pro-English in their sentiments. They tended to vote for the augmentation of the land-forces, and preferred a Stadholderate that was powerful, because they were most in danger of attack by land in the event of a European war. The neutrality which the Republic maintained in the eighteenth century was neither pro-French nor pro-English. It was pro-Dutch, and the division was not as to whether the Republic would continue neutral, but as to how best to maintain this chosen role with safety. As this role was not seriously threatened, the domestic debates on how to maintain it did look to the foreigner, who was not often entirely familiar with the way the Dutch government arrived at decisions, as if the ministers were weak and indecisive. But when a decision was required, as in 1747 (the end of the second Stadholderless regime) or in 1759 (when a considerable fleet of convoy vessels was voted, financed, equipped and got afloat within about six months), measures could be put in hand with more speed than anyone outside the Republic supposed to be possible.

As has already been explained, the accepted way round a deadlock in the decision-making process in the Republic could be an appeal to a Stadholder. Commissions to this office were traditionally given to the leading member of the House of Orange. Another of the disasters which afflicted the Republic in the eighteenth century was the way dynastic accident struck over and over again among the descendants of William the Silent. The Stadholder-King died childless. He designated the young prince of the Frisian branch of the family as his general heir. But this family had lost its adult ruler in 1696, and the surviving son (who was third in the family) was aged only fifteen when his famous cousin died. At so young an age, and without influence in the wealthy western provinces, it was impossible that Jan Willem Friso should provide any solution to the Republic's governmental problems. Moreover there was a succession question, because of the Great Elector's claims through his Orangist mother, and the disputed terms of the will of her father Frederick Henry. Jan Willem was blessed with good health, many talents and an able regent in the person of his mother. But he remained, like his ancestors, Stadholder only in Friesland and Groningen. Worse was to follow, for after a young manhood of the kind to be associated with inheritance and hopes of future power, however faint, Jan Willem was accidentally drowned in 1711. He had married Marie Louise of Hesse-Cassell, and she became the guardian of his infant son and heir. The official historian of the House of Orange awards her an honourable place among the many guardian foreign princesses who have brought up Orangist heirs. But after 1702 for many long years ahead there was not much to be hoped for by the Dutch from their former Orangist saviours.[1]

After William III died, government in the Netherlands continued in the hands of those to whom it had been increasingly entrusted when the Stadholder had become King of England. The grand pensionary, Anthonie Heinsius, and the greffier Francois Fagel

[1] N. Japikse, *De Geschiedenis van het Huis Oranje Nassau* II, (The Hague, 1938) 79–100, and see genealogical Tables III and IV facing 286.

(the Old, to distinguish him from his grandfather, 'the Oldest', and his great-nephew, 'the Young', both greffiers and both also called Francois) carried out their respective duties over very long periods. Heinsius in 1719 was re-elected, at the age of 77, for a further five years to the office of Grand Pensionary held by him since 1689, whilst Fagel, who had been co-greffier with his father between 1685 and 1690, was to hold the office himself until 1744.

The election of a new grand pensionary was a major event for the diplomats at The Hague as well as within the Republic. Heinsius suffered a stroke in July 1720 and the succession to his post, already much speculated on, became a matter of international moment. England and France, full of mutual suspicions, accused each other of trying to manipulate the election; the final choice was hailed as a victory for France. Because Hoornbeck, the new grand pensionary, was relatively unknown outside the Republic it was supposed that he had been chosen because he would be pliant towards Amsterdam and thus act in the French interest. The truth seems to lie rather in the fact that towards the end of his tenure of office Heinsius had been less successful in co-operating with the Amsterdammers than he had been earlier, and that his attitude towards a possible entry into the 'Quadruple Alliance' had made them wary of him. Dutch domestic politics, depending so much on the relations between the grand pensionary of the States of Holland and the burgomasters of Amsterdam, had more to do with the choice of Hoornbeck to succeed Heinsius, than had the direct issues of foreign policy.

When Slingelandt succeeded Hoornbeck in 1727 the Republic found itself with a grand pensionary who believed in European peace, in good order and in good government. Slingelandt had already held many offices, and had especially been instrumental in an important attempted fiscal reform in 1725.[2] But even his biographer cannot altogether clear him of being 'endowed with too much determination'[3] to work easily either with the greffier or with Amsterdam, and he was unable to bring about any governmental changes. He remained grand pensionary until his death in 1736, aged 72.

It must now be abundantly clear that there was much continuity in the tenure of the more important offices in the Republic, with the

---

[2] The year in which he was appointed Treasurer General of the Union. Goslinga, *Slingelandt*, 13.

[3] *Ibid.*

exception of the Stadholdership. But continuity brings accompanying disadvantages. Enterprise, initiative, even leadership, are not always the qualities most obviously to be found when one person occupies the same seat of office for many decades, vacating it, usually to a relative or to a long-trusted subordinate only when stricken down by illness or death. It was accepted long before the grand pensionary Heinsins died, that he would become ill whenever the States of Holland were due to convene, and that their meeting, however important, would therefore have to be postponed. The Stadholder's office being unfilled, there was no hope from that quarter. The House of Orange was, anyhow, represented by another *postnatus,* who was physically malformed, it was said as the result of a fall in infancy; and he was moreover denied, as he grew to man's estate, all experience or training in military matters by the anti-Stadholderian regime which had seized power in the States of Holland and intended to keep it. Moreover, the States attempted to ruin, by exorbitant tax demands and closures of some sources of revenue, the whole financial standing of the Orangist house remaining in the northern provinces,[4] so it was perhaps fortunate for the Republic that there was some degree of stability in Europe in the 1720s and 1730s.

This is not however to imply that the Netherlands government proceeded on its way untrammeled either by domestic or exterior problems. Domestically, around this time the Dutch became increasingly the victims of what are best described as hazards of nature. One of these was the virtual destruction of a promising economic growth point when the cattle industry became increasingly subject to *rinderpest.* There had been attacks in earlier days, but those of mid-eighteenth century and later became longer-lasting and more destructive than ever. It is estimated that 70 per cent of cattle in infected areas might be expected to succumb to the disease, and it was not until comparatively late in the century that insurance and methods of providing new stock were worked out.[5] Local disasters of such a nature involved loss of taxation revenue to the central government sometimes for long periods, because requests for relief in such dire circumstances were habitually granted.

A second natural disadvantage, which especially affected Dutch

[4] P. Geyl, *Willem IV de*, 2ff.

[5] J. A. Faber, *Cattle-plague in the Netherlands during the Eighteenth Century, Mededelingen van de landbouwhogeschool te Wageningen II* (1962), 4–5.

shipping, was the battle to keep clear of silt the big river mouths which provided access to the sea from shipyards. In previous centuries, especially in the seventeenth, the Dutch themselves had possessed the highest technological skills in shipbuilding, and the fly-boat had been the foundation of the Dutch carrying trade. But access especially to Amsterdam had always been difficult, because of the Pampus bank with its narrow shifting channel; and bigger ships had had to be loaded from, and unloaded into lighters as far away as the Texel channel and the Maersdiep. In the eighteenth century countries with clean river mouths became skilled enough to build ships of deeper draught than those which could be got to sea from Dutch yards. Unfortunately techniques of dredging did not develop as rapidly as techniques in ship-building. Amsterdam depended on horse power aboard dredging barges, by means of which mud and sand were thrown aside by bucketted wheels. The Amsterdammers also, and for many years, raised ships above the banks of the Pampus channel by fitting empty sealed tubs and barrels alongside the keels of their ships. But all this was costly, inefficient and labour-intensive; and as foreign ships were built bigger grew still less effective. These processes provided no sort of answer to increasing expertise in building ships of greater draught, capable therefore of carrying more and more cargo. By mid-eighteenth century these geographical problems of access to once-thriving Dutch ports were undermining the position held formerly by the Republic in the carrying trade of western Europe. And as revenue from shipping diminished, so did the Netherlands' ability to make a figure in Europe.

Worst of all, however, were the defensive measures which became more and more necessary, and more and more expensive, against the Republic's major enemy, the sea. As time went on, it became clear that the sea had found an increasingly useful ally in its war with the Republic. This was the mollusc *T. Navalis,* or Ship-worm, armed with a two-fold, excessively sharp shell on its forehead, and a voracious appetite for the sugar in wood-fibre. It was held at the time that this was an import from tropical waters; and its depradations had long been known as a hazard to the timbers of ships. Witte de With had used the word 'honeycombing' to describe what *T. Navalis* had done to the shields, or hoods, which were placed beneath vessels which made long voyages to tropical areas even in the first half of the seventeenth century. De With wrote in his diary for 1648–9 that nobody who had not seen the extent of this damage with his own eyes would have believed it to be possible.[6]

The damage done to wooden ships by *T. Navalis* was thus a recognized hazard. How far it was realized in the seventeenth century that attacks were also being launched by this 'pestiferous' worm on the piles supporting the dykes and other under-water woodwork in the Netherlands is not absolutely clear. In the winter of 1731 there came one of those unfortunate combinations of gale-force winds and high tides, akin to what was to happen further south in 1953, which drove the sea with colossal force on to the dykes defending districts and the polders of the Noorderkwartier and West Friesland. Catastrophic flooding resulted because the dykes did not stand against the sea's attacks. An enormous amount of damage was done; people were drowned or rendered homeless, farmland was inundated, thus impregnated with salt, whilst stock, together with seed-corn and other fruits of the previous harvest were destroyed. When the waters had begun to recede, the officials responsible for the upkeep of the ruined dykes (needless to say, this was strictly a special local authority matter, under the direction of a district organization which reported to that of the province) carried out an inspection which produced irrefutable evidence of the wooden piles being deeply infested with what was described as 'an unknown species of sea worm'. The news soon spread and reaction reached almost panic proportions. Periodicals such as the *Europische Mercurius*, with a European circulation, carried semi-scientific accounts and even illustrations, one would like to suppose only fanciful, of the damage the worm could do and what it looked like. It was even rumoured that Amsterdam was in danger of collapsing into the water, and a merchant of Abingdon wrote to his Dutch agent that he was in doubt whether or not to dispatch his usual consignment of leather goods.[7]

Preachers declared that the worm's attacks were a visitation from on high, a sign of divine displeasure.[8] More seriously, engineers,

---

[6] W. J. van Hoboken, *Witte de With in Brazilie* (Amsterdam, 1955), 5–6 and n. 9, 200, 266–7. Dr van Hoboken told me that the 'hoods' were constructed of three-fold oak planking and that de With had been absolutely horrified at what he observed when his ships were careened.

[7] Gemeente Archief Amsterdam, Brandts de Neufville Collection, 1328. I owe this reference to Dr N. B. Harte.

[8] A day of fasting and prayer was ordained. A wit proposed that the worm should be prayed to fast.

dyke-builders and all sorts of other interested persons began to consider alternative ways of defending the land from the sea, and to look at falling property-prices, failing investment incentives and other subsidiary results of the damage done to the sea-walls. Ingenious ideas such as casing piles in iron plates had to be rejected, on the twin grounds of expense and impracticability. The ultimate solution was to use stone in place of wood wherever the water was even only slightly brackish, and the expense was of course enormous. Stone had to be brought from afar, dyke-building was labour-intensive and labour had anyhow to be drafted in to reinforce local supplies, with consequent social problems. Estimates of costs, which were supposed to be as low as possible, reached totals of millions of guilders, a 'cheap' plan, using stone as sparingly as possible, worked out at well over half a million guilders for under four kilometres. Expenses on such a scale could only be met, by the local authorities responsible, if they could get exemption from central taxes, and for very many years the states of the provinces of Holland and Zeeland were being petitioned to remit contributions from the afflicted areas. For naturally once the extent of the problem had been revealed, after the breaking of the dykes in North Holland and West Friesland, inspections were made of the sea defences further south, and urgent measures had to be put in hand there also. It is reckoned that the protection of the island of Walcheren alone cost the Republic not far off three million guilders.[9] All this money had to be found somehow, and its direction into defence against the sea weakened the Republic yet further as a European power. All these costs for sea-defence were additional to the already heavy war-debt incurred since the beginning of the struggle against Spain; the Republic was carrying, we could say, vastly increased expenses of her wars not only against her human adversaries but also against her natural foe.

As well as natural hazards, during the so-called second Stadholderless regime (1702–47) the Dutch government was bedevilled by increasing corruption. Much has been made of this by Dutch historians. Few of the regent oligarchs, it is said, displayed overall patriotic feeling, their major if not only concerns being with the interests of their own localities and of their own order. Whatever the facts may be (and to generalize is still not possible, lacking as yet we do enough detailed local studies by other than

[9] A. M. Lambert, *The making of the Dutch landscape* (1971), 247.

enthusiasts or hagiographers) by the end of the 1730s we are aware
of large-scale tax-evasion, of over-emphasis on the visible
maintenance of petty local privilege and position,[10] and of over-
formalizing of patronage even in minor matters. This last was the
result of developments in the system known as 'contracten van
Correspondentie',[11] whereby powerful local families agreed to
regulate rights of nomination either to local or to provincial office.
These 'contracten' were legally binding; each family or office
holder in turn was given the right to nominate when posts were
vacated (very often only on the death of the holder). As office-
holding at every level conveyed some degree of social distinction,
nominations were nearly always confined to members of
accustomed social grades. The result was at least to slow down[12] the
rate of upward social mobility, and thus to exclude the able and
ambitious from those ranks from which such mobility was possible.
These people naturally became the breeding ground of opposition
and their talents were utilized against instead of within the
government. By the 1740s many such disappointed persons, mainly
from what we could call the sub-regent classes, had taken to
meeting in a well-known Amsterdam shooting range, had acquired
therefrom the nickname 'Doelisten' ('doel' is the Dutch word for a
'target') and were not far short of being revolutionaries.

As dissatisfaction with the ruling regime increased, a possible
alternative began to present itself to earlier supporters of the
Orangists. Willem Karel Hendrik Friso, son of William III's heir,
born in 1711, was growing to man's estate. Deprived of military
training and political influence, threatened with ruinous tax
demands and bedevilled with claims on his estate from his cousin of
Prussia, his lot had been far from happy in spite of his mother's
astuteness as his guardian. But he did represent the House of
Orange. In 1733 a marriage was arranged for him with the English
Princess Anna, eldest daughter of George II and his politically
adept consort Queen Caroline. Anna, Princess Royal of England,

[10] There was such competition to out-do former office-holders that limits had to
be set on the number of dishes to be served at inauguration dinners.

[11] The authority here is still J. de Witte van Citters, *Contracten van Correspondentie*
(The Hague, 1873) *cf*. D. J. Roorda, 'Ruling classes' in *Britain and the Netherlands* II
109–32.

[12] J. A. Faber, *Drie Eeuwen Friesland: economische en sociale outwikkelingen van 1500 tot
1800* I (Wageningen, 1972), 400 (English summary) speaks of 'a relative absence of
vertical mobility'.

did not come empty-handed, and could be regarded as a 'catch' for Willem Friso. The marriage therefore 'terribly disconcerted' those at The Hague 'who before had thwarted every Thing proposed to the Prince's Advantage.'[13] Solemnized in March 1734, on the personal side the marriage was a happy one. But politically in the Netherlands it at first proved an embarrassment. Naturally the anti-Stadholderians regarded this reforging of the link between England's ruling house and the Orangists as a threat, even if only potential. There were times when England needed Dutch co-operation, however the Republic was being ruled. When this happened there were difficulties, because the English king was now the father-in-law of someone who could be regarded as the leader of the opposition in the Republic. When the newly married Prince and Princess of Orange visited Rotterdam, The Hague and Amsterdam, they were coolly received; only when they arrived at Leeuwarden were they made welcome in style. Here for a dull frustrating thirteen years they made their home, and kept a court of a kind, getting what distraction they could from mixing with the local nobility and disputing points of protocol with the Dowager Princess of Orange. Meanwhile even when George II was passing through The Hague on visits to or from his electorate, Anna was not often able, for Anglo-Dutch political reasons, to pay her respects to him in person. And she was being obliged to observe, from her far-off gloomy eyrie, her hated brother of Cumberland becoming a general of European renown, whilst her sisters were making marriages that promised better than her own.

As time went on, however, things slowly changed for the better, from the Orangist point of view, and the Frisian couple became a little more hopeful. Increasing dissatisfaction with the rather tepid, somewhat inglorious, and undoubtedly increasingly corrupt rule of the anti-Stadholderians, would not of itself have contributed much to the future of the Prince and Princess of Orange. But there had arrived in the Netherlands the two sons of William Bentinck, Duke of Portland and close friend of William III, by his second marriage to the niece of Sir William Temple. These young men, steeped in the traditions of the Ancient Alliance of England with the Republic, would have found a career in the country of their birth a difficult matter to arrange, for the earlier Portland marriage had been fruitful. In the Republic, however, they could step easily into their father's shoes and become firm Orangist supporters. They soon

[13] *Gentleman's Magazine* III, May 1733, 272.

became the unchallenged leaders of a reviving Orangist party; the elder brother, William, found the Frisian couple a 'right-hand man,'[14] who set up an information centre which enabled his principals (and Anna was always well to the fore with her husband in their political concerns) to become acquainted with the growing opposition to the regents without appearing to be too concerned with it.

Some of the dissatisfaction felt generally with the Dutch government in the 1730s, was the result of its European policy. After the wars with France between 1689 and 1715, the Republic remained bound to the Anglo-Austrian alliance. But this did not oblige Dutch subservience to the policy, or policies, of the two by now much greater partners in the Ancient Alliance. As we have seen, the anti-Stadholderian, regent, government had returned, partly because of increasing financial difficulty, but mainly because there was no longer any need to take active steps for national defence, to the principle of profit-taking from remaining neutral. Apart from determined and on the whole successful attempts to uphold the rights of their own garrison troops in the barrier fortresses, in which from time to time an aggressive spirit was displayed, Dutch foreign policy in the 1730s concerned itself with maintaining peace. A treaty of neutrality was signed with France, and the Republic kept out of the Polish Succession War. Her example was followed by England. The neutrality of the Maritime Powers prevented the growth of this war into yet another major European affair; and the initiative here was taken by the Republic.[15] Naturally, in the course of the war, the Dutch continued to trade in ship timber between the Baltic and French ports, and with the Mediterranean, to their own advantage and to that of armies warring in Italy. For prevailing views of a neutral's rights and duties favoured 'impartial concession' to warring powers, rather than 'impartial refusal', and the Dutch as neutrals were empowered to trade with belligerents on favourable terms.

Furthermore, if England were to become a belligerent, whilst the Dutch remained neutral, Dutch merchants would pick up some of England's peace-time trade. So Walpole could use Dutch neutrality as an argument against George II's desire to bring England in on

[14] T. I. Larrey, grandson of the Huguenot writer Issac de Larrey, *of,* Carter, *Seven Years War,* 29.

[15] J. H. Plumb, *Sir Robert Walpole. The King's Minister* (1960), 289, *cf.* Wilson, *Foreign Policy,* 245.

the side of the emperor. Thus the Republic's prior agreement with France, to stay out of the Polish Succession War in return for a declaration that the Austrian Netherlands would remain inviolate, helped to limit the area of the war.[16]

Some historians still regard the withdrawal of the Maritime Powers from this war as somewhat ignoble.[17] It is true that in both countries there was a power-political angle to the decision to remain neutral. Walpole was well aware that if he added to memories of an unpopular war (and in England continental wars were always unpopular with the country gentry who contributed the unpredictable 'independent members' to the House of Commons) he would have trouble in Parliament after the 1734 general election. Indeed England had no need to assist the emperor's mid and east German objectives; her obligations concerned the Southern Netherlands, even though her king was as ever an elector at heart. And in the Republic, the anti-Stadholderian government was certainly concerned at the apparent increase of power adhering to the Orangists because of the then forthcoming marriage between the prince and the English princess royal. However, to interpret Dutch policy at this period in francophile terms, and as a reaction against the anglophile attitudes of the Orangist 'opposition', is totally unhistorical. For the Republic, at the time and under the circumstances then, neutrality was the sensible policy. The Dutch calculated that invasion of the Austrian Netherlands by France was extremely unlikely. They knew already that the French had need of their neutral shipping services. They also knew, and knew moreover that the French knew too, that any approach of French armies towards their sensitive southern frontier would create a domestic reaction that could produce incalculable results. The regents did not believe the French wanted to see another Stadholderian revolution in the Netherlands.

Not only was it thought that war with France would be unnecessary. It was also known that it would be terribly costly. The army of William III had already been run down. War debts were already very large, and the country was carrying, in order to service these, a heavy burden of taxation, mainly indirect but also direct in the form of levies on different localities. Some of this direct taxation

[16] Wilson, *loc. cit.* Note that English ministers were taken by surprise at this Dutch initiative, *ibid.*, n. 17.

[17] *cf. ibid.*, where the argument seems to imply that monetary concerns and a desire for peace would show a poor spirit.

was already, in 1733, being remitted because of the collapse of worm-infested dykes. In fact, the whole history of the newly-discovered danger to the dykes, becoming known through 1732 and 1733, propelled the Republic towards neutrality in a war the objectives of which were not really matters of immediate national concern.

CHAPTER SEVEN

The Republic During
Mid-eighteenth Century Wars

WITH the death of Charles VI, and the onset of the War of the Austrian Succession, matters became somewhat different. Under the terms of article 3 of the Barrier Treaty of 1715, the Republic was committed to sending auxiliary troops into the Austrian Netherlands should this area be attacked. But to fulfil this obligation would not involve the Republic in becoming a participant in the war. To fulfil treaty obligations of such a kind could be regarded, as was later to be made clear by the Swiss international specialist E. Vattel, as repayment of an ancient debt.[1] The Republic was therefore able to put its due contingent of troops into the field in the Austrian Netherlands against France, without any declaration of war. Moreover, as a neutral in a war in which England was totally committed, the Republic could exploit to the full the neutral-favouring terms of the long-ago Anglo-Dutch commercial treaty of 1674. She was able therefore to trade with France in all kinds of goods, including even naval stores, except actual weapons of war, without undue fear of English warships or even of privateers. And undoubtedly her assistance to England's enemy was not only profitable to France but also to her own merchants. England was by now well aware that the terms of the treaty of 1674 were serving her own interests ill. But for the time being she did not press too heavily on the Dutch trade that was being conducted to French advantage. There were some cases of

---

[1] Emmerich de Vattel, *Le Droit des Gens* (The Hague, 1758) III, ch. 6, para. 101.

captured Dutch ships. These seem however to have been mainly those in which there was reason to believe that actual weapons of war were being carried on French behalf. But the trade in naval stores between the Baltic and French dockyards was not greatly harassed; and where it was, cargoes were sold to English dockyard contractors, freight paid and the ships and crews released, a solution not unpleasing to both sides.

Thus the virtual non-participation of the Republic in the War of the Austrian Succession at first worked reasonably to Dutch advantage. But the Republic also had obligations to the government of England. Under the terms of the various defensive agreements between England and the Republic, notably those of 1703 and 1716, 6000 Dutch troops were to be sent to England's defence whenever she should be merely *threatened* with attack by an enemy power. When therefore in 1745 the famous 'men of Moidart' landed with Prince Charles Edward Stuart in Scotland, the Dutch sent 6000 of their insufficient soldiers to assist the English Hanoverian government in its apparent hour of need. They got little thanks, which was hardly surprising, for on this last occasion of the Republic's fulfilling its obligations under the terms of the Old Alliance,[2] the Dutch troops were badly led, ill-provided and very unwilling.[3] But they were sent; thus treaty obligations were fulfilled, as they had been with Austria.

The obligation to send the 6000 men, honoured by withdrawing garrison troops from the Barrier fortresses, had unfortunate consequences for the Dutch. As a result, the French renounced the terms of a favourable commercial treaty agreed with the Republic in 1739. But worst of all was the withdrawal of the entire English army placed between the French and the vulnerable southern frontier of the Republic, for to the English government the Austrian Netherlands, even the Republic itself, was naturally only a second line of defence against the Stuarts and France.

Taking it all in all the experiences of the Republic in the earlier phases of the Austrian Succession War were instructive to the then Dutch Government. Its members thenceforth saw that their 'neutral' line of policy could pay because England had on the whole

---

[2] Earlier occasions being in 1715 and 1719.
[3] *The Conduct of the Regents and Rulers of the Republic of the United Provinces* (1747), an English translation of an earlier Dutch pamphlet, available under its English title in the British Museum Catalogue, cruelly lampoons the Dutch troops sent to England in 1745.

still mainly observed the terms of the trade treaty of 1674; and Dutch merchants had certainly profited by acting as carriers for all belligerents. But they had also been made to realize that their allies, both English and Austrian, did not regard Dutch defence needs as pre-eminent. In fact it had become plain that when any threat developed, especially to the Protestant Succession in England, the Republic would be totally abandoned and left to fend for itself, but would still be held to the terms of the treaty of 1678.

As the war in the Austrian Netherlands went more and more in favour of France, tension within the Republic increased. In April 1747 the French approached close to the borders of Dutch Flanders, not it seems because they were proposing to invade the Republic but because it was thought that this would put heart of grace into the regents' peace-loving party. But things turned out very differently, and there occurred in Veere a tremendous popular uprising which spread throughout Zeeland, affected Rotterdam and thence the whole of the province of Holland, and called for rescue from the House of Orange. Orangist flags were sought out and flown from the masts of state buildings in The Hague; and by the end of the first week in May William IV had been voted captain and admiral of the forces, had become a member of the Council of State and Stadholder of most of the provinces, the others following.

This 'revolution', which in the Dutch context implies a change of government, but not necessarily accompanied by violence, was described by William IV, in a letter to Frederick II of Prussia as 'étonnante et subite'. It was accompanied by many of the semi-hysterical manifestations with which readers of Dutch history are often surprised and even somewhat repelled. The regents certainly submitted without opposition and with remarkable speed. And for a period of approximately a year William IV and his English consort had the Dutch Republic at their feet. The title of Stadholder, of all seven of the provinces,[4] was made hereditary, also in the female line,[5] and when a son was born to the princely pair in 1748 all seemed happily set for a new, and hopefully continuing, Orangist regime.

But there were many difficulties to be overcome. The submission of the regents appeared so complete that in important matters its relatively partial nature, especially in anti-Orangist Amsterdam,

[4] William III had been Stadholder of only five of the seven provinces.
[5] This related to the fact that in 1747 the only living issue of the new Stadholder was the Princess Caroline, born in 1743.

had passed unnoticed. Neither William IV nor his wife were adept politicians, and their experience in Friesland had in no way prepared them for what was to face them in the Republic as a whole. They committed almost automatically the errors associated with such persons as come from afar with acclaim to the seat of power, bringing with them their own familiars in whom they showed more confidence than was regarded as suitable by people who had formerly had things their own way. There developed around the court (and a court at or near The Hague was a new and as time went on a not over-popular spectacle after nearly half a century of regent government) a critical mood that was fostered by some outrageous extravagances, particularly on the part of the princess. Perhaps the greatest mistake made by William IV and his wife was not to realize whence their greatest support could come. The 'revolution' of 1747 had begun with a popular uprising. In the big cities, above all in Amsterdam, the sub-regent classes were in uproar against corruption of every kind displayed in the system of farming taxes, of appointing to office, of administration of military and naval affairs, in every branch of public life. In the late summer of 1748 William IV was implored to come to Amsterdam to make the kind of 'settlement' that was expected of a Stadholder when an otherwise insoluble situation had arisen. The so-called *doelisten,* with a noisy and frightening, but it seems totally responsible group of shipyard carpenters had managed to get the invitation to William agreed on by the Town Council;[6] William had only to put himself at the head of such non-regent bourgeois but basically order-loving persons to become a reincarnation in power of his famous ancestor who had fought long and bitterly with the regents of Amsterdam (but had however always recognized their ruling position.) But how could a locally-minded dignitary from a far-off country area be expected to act the demagogue, especially when so much under the influence of a consort who was rather contemptuous even of the nobility of her husband's country? William IV wrote back to his wife in The Hague that he was almost suffocated in the miserable quarters provided for him in Amsterdam, that crowds pushed in on him wherever he went, and that he was constantly given contradictory advice as to how he was to act in the cruel dilemma in which he had become trapped. His appointments to the Amsterdam ruling committees

6 Groen van Prinsterer (editor), *Archives de la Maison d'Orange-Nassau,* Sé. IV, ed. Th. Bussemaker (Leyden, 1912) I, 245–76. The prince was in Amsterdam from 2–14 September 1748.

were mistaken, his conduct whilst the cynosure of all eyes in the city was inept. And his performance in general only contributed to widen even further the gap between his house and the still most powerful and wealthy city of his country's most powerful and wealthy province.

As far as Europe was concerned, this sudden change of regime in the Republic was a matter of considerable interest. The French appear to have at first given in fairly easily. They recognized that an Orangist form of Dutch government would at least temporarily prevent them from exercising much power or influence in the Republic. But they kept a sharp eye on what was going on there, especially in Amsterdam and Rotterdam, and called for reports on every aspect of Dutch life.[7] The English were of course extremely optimistic. This development had been hoped for by the prevailing Whig politicians from at least as long ago as 1733, when the Orangist marriage had become a possibility. But it was not long before disillusionment set in, especially when the financial weakness of the Republic became obvious and the princess began in 1755 to ask for loans from her father.

Actually the change of government made little difference in practice to the foreign policy pursued by the Dutch Republic. This was partly due to the weak financial position of the new regime in the Netherlands, and partly to the poor showing the Dutch troops made against the French, who had no difficulty in capturing Bergen-op-Zoom in Dutch Brabant. George II and his ministers turned down a request from William of Orange for a loan in 1748, although this would have enabled the Republic to hire Russian troops in order to cover an augmentation of their own insufficient army. The continuation of the neutralist line in Dutch foreign policy was also due to the basic weakness of the Orangists after the first year of the new rule. But it was due above all to the fact that neutrality remained the only logical, as well as the only possible policy for the Republic in the last half of the eighteenth century. It can be argued, moreover, that the very failure of the Dutch troops to acquit themselves with credit against the French, preserved the Southern Netherlands from yet another blood-bath, and the Republic from yet another French attack. For at first England's major aim in the peace negotiations was the retention of Cape Breton Island at the north of the St Lawrence River. Had the Dutch

[7] These are to be found in the Archives du Ministère des Affaires Etrangères in Paris (Mémoires et Documents, Fonds Hollande, 23).

shown military strength in 1748, and been supported by Russian mercenaries, they might well have found themselves clearing the French from the Southern Netherlands, in order to retain for England her colonists' American prize. As it was, the English surrendered Cape Breton Island and peace was made, as we are told repeatedly, on a *status quo ante bellum* basis; and the Dutch were left with renewed rights to garrison barrier fortresses, but without much hope of imperial contributions to finance their continued performance of imperialist frontiersman duties. It is not, perhaps, generally realized that the Dutch did in fact re-garrison the barrier fortresses after the treaty of Aix-la-Chapelle. Their troops returned to the ruins of these far from strong-points in the course of 1749 and 1750. In August 1749 the States-General passed a resolution to seek help from England in obtaining a renewal of Austrian finance for Southern Netherlands defence, together with arrears of subsidy since 1744. Needless to say, neither English help nor Austrian financial contributions for this purpose were obtainable; moreover there soon developed the accustomed difficulties between civil and military authorities in the barrier towns. Meanwhile, 12,000 Dutch effectives (in an army reputedly 70,000 strong, but already well over 10,000 men short[8]) were tied up preparing to undertake duties which would have been impossible to perform, had a determined attack been launched by France upon the Austrian Netherlands. Moreover in these fortresses were depots of ammunition, guns and other military stores, representing a considerable investment on the part of the Dutch government in a purely defensive operation, which was anyway mainly on Austria's behalf. The presence of this arsenal was also regarded as in itself an incentive to enemy attack.

What part, besides continuing to fulfil their obligations under the barrier treaties, did the Republic play in the Europe of the period between Aix-la-Chapelle and the Seven Years War? Basically the answer is – very little, no forceful Dutch line in European policy emerged as a result of the change in the government in 1747. This was regarded at the time, and in effect by historians since, as weak, even blameworthy, and the Orangists were considered to have opted out in as cowardly and as self-seeking a way as had their predecessors the regents.

To understand why the Dutch remained apart, we must look first at how the Orangist rule continued. First of all, the Orangist

---

[8] L. André et E. Bourgeois (eds), *Recueil des instructions données aux ambassadeurs et ministres de France. Hollande* III (Paris, 1924), 245–6.

succession was soon faced with yet another minority. Dynastic accident struck yet once more when William IV died unexpectedly in October 1751, leaving a child of three to succeed to the title of Stadholder, now made hereditary. Arrangements for such a possibility had indeed been made, and the young Stadholder's mother, the English Princess Anna, was to act, with the title of Gouvernante. Anna was a determined, even in her way a courageous woman. But she lacked political wisdom and even after nearly twenty years had not been able wholly to adapt completely to her Dutch environment.

Moreover, as a woman the princess could hardly exercise her son's functions as captain and admiral-general of the Dutch forces. As it happened, a suitable candidate for the performance of these duties was already in Dutch service. This was Prince Louis of Brunswick-Wolfenbüttel, former general in the service of the empress queen, and brother of the more famous commander of that house, Prince Ferdinand, on the Prussian side in the previous war. Prince Louis had been inveigled into Dutch service when it had become clear that William IV was not capable of acting in his so much more effective predecessor's rôle of leader in war. The initiative in getting Prince Louis to the Netherlands had been William Bentinck's, at a time when the Ancient System of European Alliances had appeared to be about to be re-born, and when it was generally supposed that the Dutch would field an army once more and contribute as of old to the suppression of feared French hegemony in Western Europe.[9] Prince Louis drove a fairly hard bargain with the new Dutch regime, and in the next thirty years or so lived after initial difficulties quite comfortably in the Republic, first as a necessary military expert and authority, carrying the responsibility in military affairs for the minor-age Stadholder William V, later as a kind of *alter ego* in all sorts of ways for the prince, who on coming of age in 1766 made over to him many functions that William should have exercised himself. But Prince Louis was never really liked or trusted either by Princess Anna or after her death in 1759 by the States, and as time went on least of all by William Bentinck, whose protegé he had originally been.

It will now have become clear that the renewed Orangist regime was in no way capable, as it had been at the time of William III, of

---

[9] Such a situation was still envisaged as late as 1750, at least by Bentinck himself. A.M.O.N. 4me Sé. II, 90–6.

putting the Republic in force behind the anti-French so-called Ancient System of the Anglo-Dutch alliance. But there was anyway no longer a pressing national need for the Republic to become active on behalf of this alliance system. Also Dutch neutral services had again proved to be of great assistance to France, which would make France wary of arousing the age-old dread of Catholic encirclement always capable of being stimulated among the populace by a French approach to Dutch frontiers. It was moreover already being anticipated that Dutch shipping would become more and more valuable to France as French trade with the Caribbean increased in both volume and value. In fact during the interval between the treaty of Aix-la-Chapelle and the outbreak of the Seven Years War, more and more alien merchants, some of them English, were taking on Rotterdam citizenship and launching into the carrying trade of France. It was unlikely that France would again make the mistake she had made in 1747, and approach the Dutch frontier in force.

For a time after 1747 the French also found that they had lost certain personal contacts built up with some of the people on the outskirts of the previous anti-Stadholderian government. It was believed in Paris and elsewhere that through these contacts France had exercised, and could continue to exercise, considerable influence over Dutch foreign policy. When the change of Dutch government came in 1747, and William IV was raised to a position apparently more powerful than that enjoyed by any previous Stadholder, it was believed that England would be able to replace France in influencing the external relations of the Republic. But seen from the Dutch standpoint it is abundantly clear that by mid-eighteenth century controlling influences over Dutch foreign policy were in reality the great scarcity of means at the centre, combined with the total lack of manifest emergency in national defence. It is in fact difficult to avoid the impression that foreign representatives at The Hague, for reasons of their own, exaggerated their own importance on the Dutch political scene. Also, because under no circumstances could they oblige the Republic for non-Dutch reasons to take action desired by their principals, they were wont to exaggerate also the weakness and confusion that they were observing at the centres of Dutch government.

This is not to say that any form of government in the Netherlands, either before or after 1747, was at all strong. This was especially so after the death of William IV. The titular representative was a child of three, under the guardianship of an alien princess, with military functions exercised by an alien employé of the States. The princess tried to make sure that her son's service patronage rights would still be his when he came of age. This led to bitter controversies; and there were also acute difficulties because the princess at first refused to consider the possibility that she might die before her son came of age. She often mistook the niceties of Orangist rights over local patronage, because of the increasing breach between herself and William Bentinck, probably the only man who really knew very much about what these rights were. In the meanwhile, especially in Amsterdam, traditionally anti-Orangist, the anti-Stadholderians were staging a come-back, and by February 1752 the princess had lost all her husband's influence in nominations to office in that city.

Indeed, the anti-Stadholderian party was on the way to recovery well before it became clear in 1754 that the Anglo-French colonial war in North America was likely soon to break out also in Europe. What, whenever this European war should come about, would be the rôle of the Republic? William Bentinck and Orangists of his way of thinking were determined that the Republic should at any rate prepare for war. *Les neutralistes,* as the opposition had come to be called, believed that for the time being anyway this would not be necessary, and that in any case preparations should be concentrated on the equipment of extra ships of war to undertake convoy duties, not on the augmentation of the Republic's increasingly inadequate army. 'Equipment' or 'augmentation' became catchwords in the contest as to whether the Republic should observe an active or a passive neutrality in the coming war. Dutch politicians, with the exception of William Bentinck and a small number of fellow-Orangist noblemen never envisaged the Republic as an active participant; but with *either* an augmented army *or* ships for additional convoy duties, the Republic's still considerable resources could, it was assumed, be made use of *either* against *or* for France.

This rather *simpliste* interpretation of how the Republic could be fitted into the European system once Anglo-French colonial rivalry became a general war, overlooked the practical point of how equipment and/or augmentation should be financed. The Republic's general revenue was inadequate; even for the servicing of the various provincial debts there was sometimes a short-fall, depending on the amount of taxation that had to be remitted on grounds of calamity. As early as the autumn of 1753 Bentinck was alarmed by new proposals put forward by England for a renewal of the Barrier Treaty. The Dutch wanted better conditions for their trade with the Southern Netherlands, which the English were not prepared to agree. The princess and her advisers were ready to facilitate negotiations on rendering the barrier fortresses viable once more, but the Dutch were quite unable to contribute to the costs of re-fortification. If England brought pressure to bear on Austria to contribute towards rebuilding the fortresses, would she, or would she not, be prepared also to re-negotiate a commercial treaty which would favour Dutch traders? As her own merchants were also interested in trading on good terms in the Austrian Netherlands, this seemed somewhat unlikely. In the winter of 1753–54 there was a great deal of correspondence between London, Vienna and The Hague as to whether a new barrier treaty, underpinned with a commercial agreement, should be drawn up. This negotiation was carried on throughout 1754, but it was not until the end of November that Austria's total disenchantment with the barrier system became clear. Kaunitz wrote to Prince Louis that there seemed no reason why his court should continue to protect an area which was without defence, had no viable frontier and was anyway acting mainly as a front line for the Dutch Republic and England.[10] But without Austrian co-operation the barrier-policy could not be maintained.

The Dutch reaction was first to consider the possibility of seizing Austrian customs posts, collecting the duties, subtracting from the yield the amount of Austrian subsidies reckoned to be due, and handing the residue over to the Viennese agents. But this was felt to be an unduly provocative act which might break off the admittedly tenuous relations between Austria and the Republic, and the plan was abandoned. However, action of some sort had to be taken, if only to safeguard the armaments deposited in the fortresses. On 31 March 1755 Prince Louis submitted a long memorandum to the princess's Conference, suggesting that the Dutch garrison troops should be recalled, and the depots of war-like stores in the fortresses concentrated at Namur, which should remain protected as its possession was considered vital to the defence of the Republic proper.[11] It must be stressed that this withdrawal of the garrisons was recommended by Prince Louis not because he had 'deserted the

[10] A.M.O.N. 4 me Sé. II, 442.
[11] A.R.A., Fagel, 1181, 359–70, Prince Louis' report to the princess's Conference.

Ancient System', still less because he had joined 'les neutralistes' (interpretations put on his recommendation by the English) but because he was aware that the Dutch army was hopelessly run down. He also knew it to be far too scattered[12] to be of any protective value to any area, least of all to one which was ruled, as the Austrian Netherlands were ruled, by a distant power which was getting so little out of the country that it had ceased to value it.

Prince Louis's intention was to augment the Dutch army so as to bring it up to its former strength of 70,000 men. Before France could attack the Republic's immediate frontiers, Namur would have to be taken. So in planning temporarily to withdraw the garrisons from the barrier towns, leaving Namur well fortified, Prince Louis saw this as a necessary step, preliminary to the Dutch being able to fulfil obligations under treaty and to defend their own land frontiers should the unlikely need arise. The Republic might also be expected once again to have to send 6,000 troops to England, should the French promote another Stuart landing. Meanwhile, the trading towns, looking forward to profits from neutral trade, were beginning to see further arguments in favour of equipping extra ships of war. But it must be emphasized that neither the Orangists nor the anti-Stadholderians envisaged their country in anything but a subsidiary role. The Orangists saw the Republic as a minor assistant if England's Protestant Succession should be attacked once more. Their opponents were concerned to protect the trade of Dutch merchants with their ally's enemy, a trade that was authorized by treaty but which might so strengthen France that she could fight on indefinitely.

These arguments, suggestions, counter-plans and proposed forms of action were debated in and out of the princess's Conference, during the year 1755. Before the coming of the new year, the barrier system was virtually dead; as Holdernesse, secretary of state in the Northern Department, wrote to Sir Joseph Yorke, English plenipotentiary at The Hague:

'As the House of Austria will not, and the Republic cannot, take the share which they have hitherto done in the affairs of Europe, it is impossible to imagine that His Majesty will, in the present crisis of affairs . . . launch out into a still more expensive scheme.'[13]

---

[12] The Dutch had hired approximately another 12,000 of their troops to various German princes.

[13] 30 September 1755. Holdernesse to Yorke. Public Record Office, London, State Papers 84/491. *Sub datum.*

Meanwhile in the States of Holland an anti-Stadholderian move was made to enquire of France what her intentions might be in the coming war. It is clear that something along the lines of the 1733 agreement was envisaged, in which the Republic would remain neutral if the Southern Netherlands were left unattacked. But when this motion was put to the States-General, the four landward provinces, for different reasons, voted against it, and no definite policy for the Republic developed for the time being.

Also in the autumn of 1755, Yorke attempted to 'sound' the Republic about its future intentions. He received instructions to discover unofficially what would be a likely Dutch reaction if France should be observed to be preparing to land troops on England's coast. In such a case it will be remembered that the Republic would be due under treaty to send 6,000 troops to England's assistance, in transport vessels provided by the English. Yorke approached the princess's Conference, which though without constitutional validity contained all the more important of the Republic's officers. But just as deliberations in the Conference were apparently approaching a decision favourable to England, and after Yorke had written home to urge caution on his superiors, the transport vessels due from England sailed into Helvoetsluys. After this, suspicions in the Republic of the princess as an unpatriotic anglophile, naturally became even stronger than before. These suspicions were to dog her, rather unfairly, through the next four years of conflict in the Republic as to whether the Dutch should or should not take any steps to favour England or France in the war. Only after Anna's death, which took place in January 1759, could the domestic scene in the Republic be rid of tensions due to her nationality, her mistaken exercise of Orangist patronage, and her inability to understand the realities of the Dutch political scene.

The opening months of 1756 were crucial to decisions on Dutch neutrality in the Seven Years War. The final solution was for the Republic to make a declaration of intent to remain neutral, a decision finally arrived at because France made an official request to be informed of what Dutch policy would be, once war broke out, and because England did requisition the 6,000 troops. The declaration of intent to remain neutral was designed as an answer to both Paris and London. Meanwhile, France threw open to neutrals her hitherto closely reserved trade to her West Indian settlements; and England took careful note of the tone of debates in the States of Holland on the question of sending the 6,000 men. During these debates, it became clear that should England in fact be invaded on behalf of the Pretender, the Republic would certainly come to the rescue. What the Dutch were no longer prepared to do was to act provocatively towards France when it was unclear whether an attack would take place.[14]

The Diplomatic Revolution of 1756 worked in some ways to Dutch advantage. The Anglo-Prussian treaty of January was at first generally thought of in the Republic as a blow to France. That this was so is perhaps indicative of a less pro-French attitude in the Republic than we are sometimes led to believe. For the Dutch, the secret article was of importance because it excluded the Low Countries from the terms of the treaty. But there was little reaction at The Hague; and English attempts to bring the Republic into the alliance and to offer Frederick guarantees for Silesia and Glatz in return for defence if necessary against France, were sensibly resisted by the Dutch.

There was also little overt reaction to the news of the Franco-Austrian treaty of May 1756. By this time the Republic had already decided to remain neutral in any forthcoming hostilities. The change in the status of the Southern Netherlands, from territory of an enemy of France to territory owned by one of her allies, was thus less dramatic than it appeared. For any advance on the Dutch frontier by hostile French armies would still provoke a defensive reaction in the Republic whether the intervening area should be friend or foe, and a neutral Republic could still be fashioned thus into an active ally of England. As it turned out, French armies did use Austrian-owned routes to central European battle grounds, and supply-columns were sent thither even through Dutch territory, permission being given because neutrals still obeyed the rule of 'impartial concession' rather than 'impartial refusal' of assistance to belligerents. When French armies were put into Ostend and Nieuport in 1757, the Austrian and French ambassadors took care to break the news to the Dutch in a way that would give as little offence or cause for alarm as possible, and even tried to convince them that goods hitherto sent via these ports would henceforth be imported via Rotterdam.

[14] It was felt, surely understandably, that England's danger from a Stuart landing in 1756, was not on a par with the Dutch situation in 1702 or 1703. This, it will be remembered, was when the *casus foederis* of the defensive alliance of 1678, had been altered at the request of the Dutch to include preparations for attack. See Carter, *Seven Years War,* 56–66, where the making of the neutrality declaration is described in detail.

Although none of the belligerents in the Seven Years War was successful in bringing the Republic in, this is not to say that no attempts were made. The French tried twice without success to negotiate a neutral maritime league, in which the neutral powers would combine to protect their trade. The first attempt took place early in 1756 and the second in the winter of 1758–59. Neither was successful, the first because there seemed to the Dutch still to be little need for additional protection for their Baltic trade with France, two thirds of which was still getting through as late as June 1757, and the second because by the time French initiatives developed, the solution to Dutch trade disputes with England was being sought in other ways.

England had a more elaborate plan—to re-create the Ancient System, of Anglo-Austrian-Dutch alliances with Prussia doubling for Austria and a Prusso-Dutch army defending central Europe from the French. This, it was supposed, would suit Prussia well. Prussian troops would protect the Netherlands whilst the Dutch army was built up; and an augmented Dutch army would protect Prussia whilst Prussia fought England's battles in central Europe later on. The main trouble was that except for a few weeks in the summer of 1756 Frederick of Prussia was not enamoured of the plan, for he did not believe the Dutch would augment. And the Dutch, except for such keen adherents of the former alliance system as William Bentinck, wanted neither to augment their army nor to protect Frederick's western frontier whilst he developed any aims he might envisage to the east. In the end, when he finally perpetrated that favourite German mistake of moving eastward with an unsecured western flank, Frederick expressed his disgust at the Republic's ministers who, as he put it, appeared to think only as merchants. It was natural that the Dutch should object to Frederick's Saxon expedition, because just as earlier in Silesia, Dutch capital had been tempted in to develop resources there. But one feels all the same that in refusing to accept frontier guardsman duties against France for Frederick, and not attempting an augmentation of their army which would have been expensive and might have been provocative to the French, the Republic's ministers may just possibly have been thinking like Dutchmen.

As soon as the European war broke out there were clashes on the high seas between English and neutral sea captains. Most of these in the nature of things were between English and Dutch, because Dutch vessels carried a far higher proportion of French Baltic, coastwise, Mediterranean and Caribbean trade than all other neutrals taken together. But in fact the trading rights of the Dutch with England's enemies were not universally disregarded, and 'free ships' continued to mean 'free goods' over a very considerable area. Also, Dutch ships, mainly sailing from Rotterdam and often both owned and skippered by Englishmen or Huguenot French expatriates, were invaluable in continuing under Dutch neutral colours the tobacco trade of American colonies with France by means of Glasgow and Rotterdam. And Amsterdam for a time facilitated a continued wine trade between France and England. But there were certain trades in which England did feel it necessary to intervene. These were mainly the timber trade between the Baltic and French dockyards, and colonial trade between French ports and the French West Indies and Surinam settlements. The timber trade, though expressly authorized by the Anglo-Dutch commercial agreement of 1674, was by mid-eighteenth century of somewhat doubtful morality, because in theory it was supposed by that time that neutrals' activities should not prolong a war. Providing France with naval stores, especially mast timbers either unobtainable domestically, or which could not be conveyed to dockyards where they were most required, undoubtedly both prolonged the war and increased French war-potential. The opening months of the war witnessed many captures of Dutch timber ships and a near-engagement between English privateers and the convoys of a fleet of Dutch merchantmen homeward bound from the Baltic. But a reasonable solution was found when the captured ships were allowed to discharge their cargo in England, for which freight and sometimes even demurrage was paid, as well as a sum for purchase by English dockyard officials. The Dutch did not particularly care whether their goods reached the original consignees. They were after all mainly merchants, not French auxiliaries.

The real crisis in Anglo-Dutch relations did not develop until the summer of 1758. In this year, possibly to create disorder in the economy of the Caribbean preparatory to an all-out attack planned there for the summer of the following year, all neutral shipping bound to or from the Caribbean was as far as possible intercepted and brought up by English men-of-war and privateers. Dutch shipping, therefore also merchants and insurers appeared to suffer more than the rest because so much neutral shipping was Dutch. It will be remembered that trade to their West Indies settlements,

hitherto strictly reserved for their own nationals, had been thrown
open to neutrals by the French before war had broken out. This
French move was unexpected. It could also originally be regarded
as at least an extension, if not actually a breach, of the terms of the
1674 treaty: for the treaty had not taken account of the position
about areas across the Atlantic, these being of far less significance in
1674 than they had become by mid-eighteenth century. And
moreover by mid-eighteenth century her West Indies trade had
become far more important to the financial security of France than
it had been when the treaty had been signed, whilst some Dutch
merchants had since 1756 sunk considerable capital in this trade,
both in providing ships and insurance for it. So that during the
crisis of 1758–59, questions important for all sides were raised and
required solution.

The French brought all possible pressure to bear on the Dutch to
continue engaging in their Caribbean and Surinam trade. They
even wanted the Republic's merchants to trade with their St
Lawrence settlements. English ministers regarded Dutch
participation in French colonial trade as something that had to be
stopped, and as an abuse of neutral rights, even of the principle of
'free ships, free goods'. The Dutch government was above all
anxious to prevent a situation in which merchant grievances could
so animate feelings in the trading towns that the Republic would be
stampeded into a declaration of war against England. There is
moreover no doubt whatever that some Dutch ship-captains were
resorting to fraud, using double ships' papers and false bills of
lading, suborning witnesses when an Admiralty Court case was on,
all the devices by which the man of the sea attempts to defeat the
landsman's law. There is equally no doubt that many privateers
were not far off being pirates, that their letters of marque were
obtained by corrupt means and that under-capitalization among
them was rife. This meant that damages and costs awarded against
them in Admiralty Courts were unobtainable. Pitt's Privateers' Act
of 1759 should have been passed early on in the war, for it put some
of these matters right, especially by exacting a substantial bond from
applicants for letters of marque. But the whole crisis proved that
some kind of settlement had become urgently necessary; both
governments were eager to arrive at one, but the problem of
negotiating on such an inflammatory matter was acute.

This matter was inflammatory in the Republic because of the
political tensions between the Orangists, supposedly, under the

English princess gouvernante's direction, altogether anglophile, and the more vocal and financially involved of the merchants in the main sea ports. In between were the more responsible of the Dutch ministers, among whom the grand pensionary of the States of Holland must be included. In the end, a seemingly weak, but actually profitable and above all extremely sensible solution was come to, for both sides tacitly agreed to allow, not a settlement but a set of legal guide-lines, to be hammered out in the English Admiralty Courts. Just before the death in January 1759 of the princess gouvernante, it was proposed in the Republic to send to England three specially commissioned officers, ostensibly to assist ships' captains and owners to present their cases at law. In reality these commissioners were so empowered to select the cases they advised on that Dutch merchants would be able to see which trading opportunities could be engaged in without interference from English ships. Similarly, the timing and the order in which cases came up in the English Admiralty Courts was managed to the same end. As each class of captured ship was dealt with, out-of-court settlements took place between owners and captors in cases similar to that in which judgment had been pronounced. Thus capital assets, in the shape of ships, cargo and skilled personnel could be unlocked, and insurance claims brought nearer to solution. These crucial judgments in the Admiralty High Court were given in the course of 1759 and early in 1760. Thereafter Dutch trade, conducted along lines that would not be interrupted, increased again and prospered.

What in effect these court judgments established was the so-called 'law of the War of '56'. After March 1760, when this law was clearly stated from the Dutch side (Holdernesse had first put clearly the principle of this law in a letter to Yorke of 29 August 1758) it was recognized as unacceptable that subjects of a neutral power should be permitted to trade during war in areas from which they were excluded in peace time. France had thrown open her West Indies' and other colonial trade to the subjects of neutral powers just before the Seven Years War broke out. She even considered allowing neutrals to continue this trade for three years after peace should have been made. In this she was innovating, in order to be certain that her valuable colonial trade would be covered, without having to stretch her maritime resources too far. After 1759 the Dutch and other neutrals at least knew where they stood with regard to such trading ventures, and it should be realized that at this time the Dutch government accepted these limitations as just. They were not prepared to defend nationals whose activities increased the war-potential of belligerents. In other words the Dutch wanted to remain correctly neutrals, convoying only their own legitimate trade. For this purpose the equipment of 25 extra war ships was voted at the instigation of the Province of Holland, and 21 were brought into service with commendable speed. But they were used for defensive, i.e. convoy purposes, not for attack as the French had perhaps half hoped. It is a mistake to suppose that during the Seven Years War Dutch neutrality was French-orientated.

CHAPTER EIGHT

The Last Years of the Dutch Republic

Economic Decline and Continuing Non-Alignment In the quarter-century or so that elapsed between the Peace of Paris and the outbreak of the French Revolution, Europe underwent considerable change and development. There was a great, though uneven, acceleration of population growth. There was a dramatic increase in the rate of economic enlargement, above all in overseas trade. There were significant technological changes in some areas, including ship-building. On the international scene there was a shift of interest and concern from west to east, and England for a time virtually deserted the European stage. Above all there were changes in the realm of ideas, particularly in thinking about social structures; especially the process of aristocratization that had marked the earlier years of the eighteenth century began to be reversed, in fact the process began to merge into something like genuine democracy.

In the Dutch Republic these tendencies were not all to be descried. Population growth proceeded very slowly. Overseas trade and the economy did not increase but suffered a decline. There were few if any technological advances. Even in the financial sector, where the Dutch had earlier ruled supreme, their techniques, having been copied by outsiders, were improved upon elsewhere, notably in London. And the silting up of Dutch harbour mouths prevented the building and getting to sea of ships comparable in size to those of countries which had begun earlier to rival the Dutch as international carriers. By the end of the eighteenth century the average Dutch merchantman was four Amsterdam, i.e. just under five, feet shallower in draught than its rivals.

Internationally, events for a time enabled the Republic, like England, to withdraw, and to pursue undisturbed her chosen policy of non-alignment. This was partly because the Austro-French treaty of 1756, revised in 1757, continued, so that the Southern Netherlands remained the territory of an ally of France. With the decreasing credibility of the Stuart cause, this removed from the scene the bogey of dynamic Catholic encirclement which had earlier cemented the alliance between the Republic and England.

Another reason why at least temporarily the Republic felt able to remain unaligned was Frederick of Prussia's concern with his eastern ambitions. And as time went on a third reason for maintaining strict neutrality began to come to the fore. This was the probability of reaping still further rewards from the twin Anglo-Dutch treaties of the 1670s which had not been in any way re-negotiated, but merely interpreted, by the English Admiralty Court decisions of 1759. For as time went on disputes between England and her North American colonists became more and more frequent; and so did Dutch shipments of naval stores and other so-called 'warlike materials' to North America and to their West India islands. At St Eustatius in particular a whole depot of such goods began to be built up. We will return shortly to this theme.

In the area of thinking about changes in social structure, in the approach to something almost recognizable as democracy, the Dutch contribution was considerable. There were many reasons why this should have been so. Since the later decades of the seventeenth century the United Provinces had become more subject to a rapid growth in the process of aristocratization than elsewhere, perhaps because there was further for leaders of Dutch society to go in that direction than there was elsewhere. After all, if aristocrats are an élite, and wealthy merchants can be categorized, like county gentry in England, as élite-minus-one, there were numerous very wealthy merchants in the seventeenth-century Republic. One finds the sons of these merchants, whose fathers had been content to dwell in part-warehouses along the main quays of their native towns, building magnificent dwelling houses and furnishing them in the best French style of Versailles; or honest dark brick facings were replaced with Palladian-style pillars; even a move made into the country to a parked residence built on the model of those of French or English nobility. Local responsibilities were relegated to subordinates or substitutes and hunting replaced trade as a day-to-day occupation. French life-styles were copied and French became virtually the only language of polite Dutch society.

All this was familiar throughout eighteenth-century Europe. But in the Republic the not-so-distant forbears of the new Frenchified aristocratic families had had a more democratic tradition than elsewhere. Their leaders had hitherto been regarded as the guardians, not, as their grandsons were to become, subvertors of privilege. And the gulf between the beneficiaries of upward social mobility, and those who whilst not much less wealthy, nor much less powerful, had been much less fortunate in their forbears' progress up the ladder to wealth and influence, created tremendous social tensions among Netherlanders towards the end of the eighteenth century. Penetration into the families of the ruling oligarchy became virtually impossible except through the fortunes of marriage. Moreover, within the 'aristocratized' area there remained the age-old divisions between Orangists and anti-Stadholderians, and the age-old divisions also between ruling families within each party. It is not therefore surprising to find that in so literate and so avidly a pamphleteering and book-buying country as the Republic, there were many publications at all levels condemning the way that more and more wealth, and greater and greater privilege appeared to be falling into the hands of fewer and fewer people. The intellectual heirs of the former 'doelists', prominent in the 1740s became leaders of the so-called 'Patriotten' of the 1770s and '80s, when there occurred an actual though short-lived revolution. These people met, formed clubs, wrote and addressed the public in the traditional Dutch manner and their condemnation of their own society found many echoes elsewhere. Thus through the writings of the Patriots the Republic did make a contribution to Europe's intellectual growth during the period leading up to the French Revolution.

On the international political scene in the 1760s the Dutch, though inactive, remained watchful. To the south, though France and Austria were now allies, there still remained Dutch garrisons in the barrier fortresses on the border between the Austrian Netherlands and France. There were still therefore, Austro-Dutch difficulties in connection with these. There were still disputes about Calvinist worship in these Catholic areas. The problems about trade and about supplies for the garrisons remained. Relations between civil and military authorities continued tense. Moreover the Scheldt remained closed by tariff barriers against all but Dutch or Dutch-allied merchants, with moreover after 1715 international guarantees.[1]

Moreover, the Vienna-Versailles axis created difficulties along the eastern frontier between the Republic, Prussia and the encircling bishoprics further south. Earlier, the multiple nature of that frontier had proved its own prophylactic, since there had been counterbalancing interests between neighbouring powers. But by mid-eighteenth century the situation had changed. Previously Prussia had pressed dangerously, partly because of the dynastic link between the houses of Orange and of Hohenzollern. But by mid-eighteenth century Prussia was primarily interested in eastern developments and, although Emden had become completely Prussian, the Dutch could for the time being look calmly from Defzÿl across the Dollart Sea. But now that Vienna and Versailles were linked, it seemed possible that a majority, if not all, of the senior ecclesiastical appointments further south, whether episcopal or administrative, might fall into the hands of persons who favoured France. This could present a danger of French pressure at a new point on the Dutch frontier. There is a mass of correspondence, memoranda, reports from minor agents and even of spies on this possible threat.[2] But on the whole, the situation was contained, no open attack developed and the knowledge acquired in the course of these enquiries enabled the Dutch ministers to maintain reasonably good relations with both the bishops and other German princelings.

There were also good relations with the King of Prussia. A year after coming of age in 1766, William V of Orange married a niece of Frederick the Great. So by the end of the 1760s we can say that the Republic was still able to feel confident in her non-alignment. For her anxieties to the south were allayed because the Franco-Austrian alliance continued, and the Stuart cause being virtually non-viable, the English Protestant Succession seemed secure. A watchful eye was kept on the bishoprics to the east, and through the Orange-

[1] Bindoff, *Scheldt Question,* esp 135.
[2] A.R.A. Fagel, esp. 1420–24, 1431.

Hohenzollern marriage the Republic had perhaps agreed with a possible adversary in Prussia. Anyhow Prussia seemed not to be greatly interested in furthering any western objective and to have plenty on hand in the east.

In terms of real strength, however, there is no doubt that by the end of the 1760s the Republic was becoming weaker. The major domestic issue between Orangists and anti-Stadholderians still turned on the questions of whether the Dutch army should be augmented or whether extra ships of war should be equipped for convoy duty were it presently again to become necessary to protect Dutch merchantmen. So traditional a cause of disagreement, stemming even from the days when William II in 1650 had tried to bludgeon Amsterdam into agreeing to keep the Dutch army in being after 1648, divided the wealthy 'maritime' from the remaining four 'landward' provinces. The landward provinces still had a majority in the States-General, but became less and less able to take an initiative that required means to implement it because wealth was still so overwhelmingly in the hands of the maritime provinces. The resulting governmental deadlock at the centre intensified the miseries of increasing economic decline, which by the end of the 1760s had already in some areas passed from its 'relative' phase into its 'qualitative' and even in some aspects into its 'quantitative' phase. This decline prevented the Republic from taking an active, let alone any major, part in shaping the new Europe of the eighteenth century. It also had a marked and most depressing psychological effect. There grew up a morbid mood of self-doubt, even of despair, to which two major financial crises, that of 1763 and another ten years later, contributed much. There was also lacking any realization of why economic decline had set in, coupled with total inability to deal with its causes or to better the situation in any way. Hopes that the whole of the economy could be revitalized by rebuilding Amsterdam's former importance in the entrepôt trade or that worth-while enterprises could be financed by repatriating capital invested abroad proved illusory. A lot of money, and much expertise, was put into attempted drainage of the area south of Rotterdam and along the line of the River Lek. But returns on capital, if any, were minute; thus proprietors' losses and the dashing of many hopes merely contributed to depression. These unsuccessful and old-fashioned ideas produced a general feeling that things could only continue to go from bad to worse.

There was also an increasing lack of leadership. Let us look first at what happened, after the death of Princess Anna of Hanover, to the ten-year-old hereditary Stadholder William V, aged only three when his father died in 1751. The princess had wielded power in her son's name until her death early in 1759, exercising all but his strictly military and naval duties. On her death these powers were divided (by agreements made earlier with each of the seven different provinces) between Prince Louis, who became William's personal guardian, and the provincial states who received back their former powers of patronage and nomination. When William V attained his majority he registered an 'Act', so-called, 'of Consulentship' in favour of Prince Louis in which, among other things, Prince William agreed only to 'consult' Prince Louis, in whom he declared his complete and utter confidence. Virtually the whole direction of Orangist affairs was thus vested in this foreign military expert, who had first come to the Republic as an employé to assume command of the Dutch forces. His was indeed a surprising career, and the motives behind the slow but sure way in which Prince Louis inexorably gathered into his own hands almost all the decision-making powers that had remained with the House of Orange is a story not yet fully told. From 1766 onwards, with only a few exceptions, William V submitted his judgment totally to that of Prince Louis, whose motives for achieving such a position have variously been interpreted as a coup which brought him full power, as an indication of the Stadholder's weakness and lack of energy or interest, and even as a selfless assumption by Prince Louis of a burden almost too heavy to bear, shouldered for love of the Republic in view of what was supposed to be William V's 'incapacity', even 'viciousness', of which it was said the prince was only too well aware. The overall result was, needless to say, that the prince himself became yet another party leader within the Orangist ranks. On the death of the grand pensionary Stein in 1772, his replacement was van Bleiswijk, hailed as a 'creature' of Prince Louis. And the Princess of Orange, niece of Frederick the Great, was also, it must be noted, a niece of Frederick's brother-in-law, no less a person than Prince Louis of Brunswick.

In the anti-Stadholderian party there were not divisions so much as developments that further fractured decision-making by the Dutch political machine. One was the increasing withdrawal of burgher patriciate families from the towns. Even early in the eighteenth century it was being surmised that Amsterdam, like

Venice, would come to resemble a museum of stones, bereft of active business because its leaders had left it.[3] There was also a steady increase in the number of offices monopolized among the leading families by the system of *contracten van correspondentie* and further formalization of the process by which local offices were filled by family members and their immediate hangers-on. Coupled with the effects of longevity and, to be fair, a tradition that to opt out of public service was in some sense ignoble, we get a grand pensionary, Heinsius, who at the age of 77 was looking forward to a further five-year term of office, and an important public post, that of greffier, held over many years by successive members of one family alone, that of the Fagels. Moreover, as elsewhere office, when attained to, became regarded as part of personal property (and some posts could even be bought or sold). This could mean that the incumbent's immediate concern would be to ensure that the succession passed to the favourite, whether son, son-in-law, nephew or grandson, if not of the holder or of his kinship, at least of one of his social grouping. By the last quarter of the eighteenth century these customary ways of appointing to office, with an overtone of office as personal property, had become perpetuated in the Netherlands and constituted one of the outstanding social grievances against which the *Patriotten,* successors to the earlier Doelists, rebelled.

Another development among anti-Stadholderian merchants, especially in Amsterdam and Rotterdam, resulted from the failure in 1759 to re-negotiate the treaties of 1674 and 1678, or even on England's part specifically to assert their interdependence. Because these treaties still held, there remained the expectation of profit to be made out of maintaining a strict neutrality, when combatants in any actual or forthcoming war required what were now defined as 'war-like materials', regarded as equivalent to the 'war-like stores' which under the 1674 treaty were free.

In the 1770s Dutch trade with North America, inhibited by the English blockade, soon brought the United Provinces on to the international stage again. So far, Dutch rights were still limited only by the definition of contraband, confined to actual weapons of war, in the treaty of 1674, and by the unilateral, rule-of-thumb 'law of

[3] Montesquieu wrote of Amsterdam in 1729 'Je vois qu'il en sera comme à Venise où, au lieu des Flottes et de royaumes, il reste de beaux palais'. *Voyages* II, ed. 1894–6, 222.

the War of '56[4] used as a guide-line in the English Admiralty Court decisions of 1759 and 1760. Moreover, English ministers had never yet specifically underlined their view that if the Dutch refused the armed assistance provided for by the defensive alliance treaty of 1678, England would not be bound by the terms of the commercial treaty of 1674. And anyhow increasing sophistication of warlike weaponry and techniques had hopelessly outdated the 1674 treaty's distinction between 'warlike stores' and actual weapons, whilst it was generally accepted, it seems, that the 1678 treaty did not apply to a war between a home country and colonists.

A further unsolved problem was how to draw up sets of ships' papers which should be proof against fraud. Even Lord Hardwicke's legal wisdom and drafting abilities had proved unequal to this task, although he had had the difficulty in mind as early in the Seven Years War as 1756. By the end of the 1770s there were legal luminaries in Amsterdam and Rotterdam who had become adept at changing ships' nationalities almost overnight.

With so many questions, vital to the continuation especially of an unarmed neutrality, still awaiting solution, and with Dutch merchants as determined as ever to pursue their still lawful trade, it is hardly surprising that even before war broke out there should have been much activity on the diplomatic front between England and the Republic. By 1775 the Dutch were already supplying weapons of war direct to the North American colonies, and also stocking up their own West India islands, especially St Eustatius, with guns and ammunition in quantities far greater than their normal requirements. But until war actually broke out these merchants were not in breach of any treaty agreement; and as far as the requirements of their own colonies were concerned labour relations were already becoming difficult and planters' needs for armaments therefore arguably greater than previously. There begins to emerge from a study of Anglo-Dutch diplomatic exchanges, even as early as 1774, much the same pattern as in the previous war – attempts by central government officials to limit merchant enterprise in supplying this time not the French but the American need of arms in the interests of maintaining good relations with England. And until the colonists were actually at war with their mother-country, and France had embraced their cause

---

[4] Later well expressed by James Madison in the title *An Examination of the British Doctrine which submits to capture a Neutral Trade not open in time of Peace* (America and London, 1806).

and therefore become England's enemy, one is hard put to it to see why Dutch merchants should be accused of being treaty-breakers who ought to have been dealt with 'firmly' *ab initio*.[5] The wisdom of such activities, in view of the fact that the Republic's neutrality was still virtually unarmed, is a different matter.

The weakness of this unarmed neutrality was inherent in the struggle between the party of the Orangists and that of the anti-Stadholderians. By 1775 the burning issue of whether the military or the naval forces of the Republic should be increased had reached a new crisis. After the events of the early spring of that year in Massachusetts, England requested from the Republic the return of the so-called Scots regiment,[6] which had been in Dutch service since the end of the sixteenth century. Even the Dutch government, and of course the merchants regarded this request as a means by which England could obtain auxiliary troops from the Netherlands, even though the 1678 treaty, giving England 6000 men from the Republic in case of attack, did not apply outside Europe or to a war between a mother country and her colonies. The Orangist party, with its increasing overtones of militarism, eventually gave way over this question and was anyway becoming weaker as the democratically-minded *Patriotten* evinced greater and greater sympathy for the ideals of the American colonists. Whilst not in general in any way allies of the mercantile old-style anti-Stadholderians of the major sea ports, like them the *Patriotten* were ranged against the Orangists, who were thus facing in the later 1770s two different enemies. In 1777 the equipment of further convoy vessels was voted, a defeat for the Orangists in the States-General, yet in numbers barely adequate for the needs of Dutch traders, now that England and her colonies were at war, and powerful England therefore vitally concerned to put down any trade in armaments or in warlike stores with North America or the West Indies.

The Fourth Anglo-Dutch War, 1780–1784   War was not declared between England and the Republic until 20 December 1780. In the

---

[5] Daniel A. Miller, *Sir Joseph Yorke and Anglo-Dutch Relations 1774–1780*, (Mouton, The Hague, 1970) *passim*.

[6] This small army had been retained in Dutch pay since 1592 partly as a result of negotiations over the liability of the new United Provinces for expenses of English assistance during the Revolt. By the eighteenth century recruiting for this regiment was permitted in Scotland. There are plenty of Dutch families with Scots surnames as a result.

years leading up to the declaration, events began to move fast in the Republic, by way of contrast to the slow-motion of the '60s and the earlier '70s. In particular, the issue of whether the Dutch army, or the Dutch fleet, should be added to, became once more the major political battle-ground, as earlier, between the Orangists and the anti-Stadholderians. This matter remained at first a prestige affair; but after France came into the war on the side of the Americans in 1778, it became a burning issue.[8] The States-General, always moderate, felt they should stand by earlier definitions of 'permitted' trade, and accept that actual weapons of war were contraband. A stand was also taken against providing 'unlimited' (onbeperkt) convoy for Dutch trade, without any guarantee that goods on board were 'permitted', or that ports of destination were not 'enemy' blockaded. Thereupon France put a stop to her trade with all Dutch towns except Amsterdam and Haarlem, whose representatives in the States of Holland had spoken up for 'unlimited' convoy. In the meanwhile, a meeting had taken place in Aachen between some Amsterdammers and Americans who were interested in a possible trade treaty.

At the same time difficulties over Dutch Caribbean trade were enhanced because the governor of St Eustatius, Johannes de Graaff, was said to have ordered Dutch ships to recognize the American flag, had taken no steps to hinder an American privateer who had seized an English ship almost within the harbour mouth and had failed to reply to friendly overtures from governors of nearby English islands. He had also, according to Sir Joseph Yorke, allowed American ships to use harbour facilities available at St Eustatius.[9]

In 1779 England made a formal request, as in 1745, 1756 and 1759 and earlier, for the help due from the Republic under the terms of the treaty of 1678, but without success. She therefore in the spring of 1780 declared unilaterally that the terms of the commercial treaty of 1674 would be considered to have lapsed. This was of course tantamount to a declaration of all-out attack on such Dutch trade as could in any sense be considered of assistance to

[8] On this matter, the authority is J. S. Bartstra, Jr., *Vlootherstel en legeraugmentatie,* a 'key' work for the understanding of Dutch domestic politics in the period leading up to the fourth Anglo-Dutch war, unfortunately still untranslated into English and therefore largely ignored by other than Dutch writers on the period.

[9] A collection of documents on de Graaff's governorship of St Eustatius is to be found in A.R.A., Fagel, 1433.

England's adversaries. Other factors contributing to the outbreak of the war were the activities of the American privateer Paul Jones, who took refuge in Dutch waters against the danger of capture by English warships, and was hailed as a hero by the Dutch, who refused to surrender him and his ships to their still so-called ally. Then in September 1779 the results of the Amsterdam–American discussions held at Aachen the previous year, in the form of a suggested draft trade treaty between the Republic and the colonists in revolt, fell into the hands of the English government.

On the Dutch side there were also many reasons why the fourth Anglo-Dutch war came about. By the late 1770s Dutch traders hoped to profit from France and feared England for she was endangering even more than before what they still regarded as their legitimate trade. Pares' 'Anglo-Dutch crisis' of 1758 had been re-born in a guise more threatening than before. There was also among Dutch statesmen some perception of the fact that their virtually unarmed country was by now being pressed upon not only by France but by other powerful western European countries and that it might become necessary, in order to retain independence, to desert the non-alignment which had earlier served them fairly well. Earlier experiences on the eastern frontier had shown that a multiplicity of greedy neighbours could be overcome by making alliances with some against others or by promoting coalitions among roughly equivalent hostile groups and thus preserve the Republic from attack by either or any. To the south, the danger from the one overmastering opponent, France, had at first been met by anti-French coalitions, notably those engineered by the Stadholder-King. But when France became merely one among several of the Republic's enemies, the principles hitherto applied to the eastern frontier, could now perhaps be used also to defend that to the south. It might even become politic to ally *with* France, especially once France became the ally of England's colonists against their mother country. Moreover by then it was Great Britain that needed to be weakened, as she had become an almost overwhelming threat to the Dutch in the Far East, where Dutch interests were vital to the maintenance of such economic strength as remained to the Republic. England was also the villain of the piece over Dutch trade across the Atlantic and to the Caribbean. There thus developed a stronger move than ever in some merchant circles in favour of an overt alliance with France.

Not only the merchants and less forcefully the thinking politicians were in favour of a change in foreign policy from neutrality towards commitment. Dutch intellectuals were also investigating some French but primarily English enlightenment ideals and beginning to see in a general movement towards something coming to resemble popular sovereignty, a hope that their country might once more become great. Before the outbreak of the French Revolution, French enlightenment ideals did not bear very much on thinking about alliances or on Dutch foreign policy. But especially among intellectuals there grew up the feeling that the accustomed recipients of power in the Republic, the Stadholder and his noble supporters, and the traditional regent families in the big towns, were clearly losing the confidence of the people among whom traditionally there remained the right to delegate power. Dutch intellectuals, whose leaders were such people as Joan Derk van der Capellen and others of the by now so-called *Patriotten* were concentrating in their writings, speeches, and, typical of Dutch political life, in their clubs and discussion groups, on ideas thought to have been current at the time of that Netherlands 'finest hour', the revolt against Spain. To already-fashioned, strongly held and passionately promulgated traditions about Spanish cruelty, tyranny and denial of privilege, were added attitudes about popular sovereignty, Teutonic freedoms, and the duty of rulers to resign if popular confidence were to be withdrawn. Montesquieu, though not, it seems, Rousseau, was already well-studied by Dutch intellectuals along with Locke, Price and Priestley, a good couple of decades before the events of July 1789.[10] And indeed it was patently obvious in Dutch government circles that power was being abused. Neither the Stadholder, with his noble supporters, nor the regents, who included the leaders of the opposition to the Stadholder though also some of his supporters, were capable of providing leadership or the remotest sense of national identity or purpose.

Before the outbreak of the fourth Anglo-Dutch war, the Republic had taken one step away from the neutral towards the aligned position in international relations. It will be remembered that in the Seven Years War the French, who then as well as later were dependent on neutral shipping services for naval construction

---

[10] A brilliant short discussion of the Dutch intellectuals' position at this time is accessible in I. Schoffer, *Short History,* section 17, 102–6. On a bigger scale *cf.* E. H. Kossmann, 'The crisis of the Dutch state 1780–1813: Nationalism, Federalism, Unitarism' in *Britain and the Netherlands* IV, eds. J. S. Bromley and E. H. Kossmann (The Hague, 1971), 156–75.

material and for getting home colonial produce, had twice tried to promote armed leagues of neutral powers. In that period the Dutch had not so great a need of protection against belligerents, especially English, privateers, because they were aware that England would not press too heavily on their carrying trade, for fear of cementing a Franco-Dutch alliance. But twenty years later things were different. The other neutral powers, especially the Baltic powers, were stronger than previously, so that the whole burden of convoying neutral merchantmen was not so likely to fall on the Dutch. The Russian Empress and her advisers might make an adequate focal- point for such an organization, whereas previously a firm lead (and over this matter Catherine was indeed firm, at least at the beginning) had been hard to seek.[11] Moreover, the necessity for trade-protection was now greater than ever because trade was being carried on on a larger scale even than in 1758, Caribbean waters were even more disturbed and English privateers now more numerous, larger and infinitely better-armed than they had been twenty years before. From the English point of view it is quite obvious why Sir James Harris, then England's envoy plenipoten- tiary at the Russian court, should have received instructions to do everything in his power to prevent the Dutch from adhering to the Armed Neutrality.

In this, however, Harris did not succeed, for the Dutch joined the Armed Neutrality ten days before the fourth Anglo-Dutch war was declared. But as the league was unsuccessful from the neutrals' point of view, was anyhow useless for the Republic once war had broken out with England, and indeed proved a major embarrassment for Catharine the Great, the fact that the Dutch did join is mainly interesting as an illustration of new trends in the Republic's foreign policy. Dutch adherence to the Armed Neutrality shows how merchant feelings of hostility to English privateers, which twenty years ago had been prevented from developing into anglophobia, had now drawn the Republic into an anti-English international agreement. We can now recognize a half- step towards limited commitment, from the determined non- alignment of the previous sixty-odd years.

The Republic emerged with enormous losses, especially in shipping, from the fourth Anglo-Dutch war. This was partly

[11] The authority here is Isabel de Madariaga, *Britain, Russia and the Armed Neutrality of 1780: Sir James Harris's mission to St. Petersburg during the American Revolution* (New Haven, 1962), especially 216–38.

because her strength in fighting ships was mainly in frigates, suitable for convoy duty and capable of being got to sea even from ship-yards where the outlet was in process of being silted-up. There were only about 17 Dutch ships-of-the-line, that is ships capable of taking their place in the line of battle and having not less than 50 cannon on board, as against Great Britain's total of 122 such ships. And it is not clear how many of these 17 Dutch vessels were so heavily gunned as to be classifiable as 'first-raters'. Even so, the addition of the Dutch fighting sea-power to Great Britain's naval adversaries was a serious embarrassment, and an interesting contrast in view-points is gained by reading about this war first in English and then in Dutch sources. There is no doubt that the Dutch navy was much the weaker of the two. All the same, the major naval engagement between the two powers, that off the Dogger Bank in 1781, was regarded by the British as 'an expensive draw'. To the Dutch, it represented if not an outright defeat at least a major weakening of their position, for the Dutch convoy vessels had to signal the merchantmen under their charge to make back to the Baltic ports from which they had emerged, and in which the bulk of them had to over-winter. This meant unfulfilled delivery agreements with French dockyards (the cargoes being mainly naval stores), therefore penalty clauses in contracts became operative, and perhaps more important, a branch of Dutch trade had become demonstrably risky, therefore more expensive to insure and harder to capitalize. Britain was clearly now able to 'rule the seas'.

The other serious weakening of the Republic's trade resulting from the fourth Anglo-Dutch war was the loss for the time being of St Eustatius, focal point of the Dutch Caribbean trade and captured by Rodney early in 1781. The island surrendered almost without a shot fired; within the harbour was a convoy of some thirty merchantmen; and a Dutch fighting ship of 60 guns was also taken.[12]

To the Dutch merchants, the loss of many ships, with cargoes, crews and skilled *super cargoes* all at one time was very serious. There was also once more the insurance angle. Not only ships and cargo, but also key personnel were insured, by then as far as is known mainly in Amsterdam and Rotterdam; and failures of insurance *companies,* now the rule rather than the exception, as they had been

[12] P. Mackesy, *The War for America* 1775–1783 (1964) 416–8. Warehouses ashore at St. Eustatius were also as always well-filled.

twenty-five years previously, became more numerous. Moreover, St Eustatius being no longer available as the centre of Dutch Caribbean trade, the whole rhythm of this trade was for the time being disturbed. Without the island's highly prized harbour facilities some ships were even laid up in neutral ports; the accompanying evils (to the owners of both ships and cargo) of wasting capital assets present an effect reminiscent of what had happened twenty-five years before. It is ironic to reflect that shortly afterwards the island of St Eustatius was reconquered, this time by the French, together with a considerable sum of money for payment to the English forces.

The effects of the defeat in the fourth Anglo-Dutch war on the Netherlands' European standing were not as catastrophic as might have been expected. Domestically, the results were, however, considerable. Above all, the standing of the Orangists was devalued yet further. The Stadholder was, after all, by tradition the captain- and admiral-general of the Dutch land and sea forces. The Dutch army had played little or no part in the war, and the navy proved inadequate, both in numbers and in fighting power, to the demands made upon it. It was inevitable that the House of Orange should be regarded as having failed to live up to its past. Whether it was in fact due to the personal failings of William IV, of his widow the princess gouvernante or of their son William V, the record of the princely house since its recall to power in 1747 had been anything but glorious. It had become clear that the house was no longer capable of dealing with national emergency in the tradition of William I or William III. William V lived withdrawn from the bulk of his people, isolated from political reality and surrounded by English and German influences, only able to assert himself in minor matters.

The decade of the 1780s saw remarkable changes in the Netherlands, both in domestic and in foreign affairs. On the domestic front, the disasters of 1781 called forth a stirring pamphlet, *To the People of the Netherlands* afterwards discovered to be from the pen of the 'father' of the Patriot party, Joan Derk van der Capellen. In this pamphlet van der Capellen expressed a high degree of nationalist feeling, outraged by the humiliating defeats of the year of publication. There was not as yet in the Patriot creed a definitive radicalism or a programme for democratic action. There was more a call for return to the 'good old days', to an attempt 'to replace stone after stone in the decrepit building of the Republic, without changing its constitution'.[13] The immediate impact of van der Capellen's pamphlet was, however, considerable. Hitherto scattered and disparate groups of *Patriotten* quickened their efforts to co-ordinate local activities, laying plans for setting up Free Corps of armed adherents, somewhat along the lines of the urban militia bands (which even in the seventeenth century, when not needed for actual defence, had become socially desirable clubs for the wealthy and distinguished, not therefore in any sense 'Free'). What must not, however, be forgotten, was that all this activity, although inter-provincial federation of Patriot efforts was envisaged, was still founded on the long-lived provincial, even urban independent local loyalties into which the Republic had always been divided.

It is this historical bias towards provincialism and localism which makes the Patriot movement so hard for outsiders to comprehend. One must bear in mind that sovereignty, as well as local loyalties lay primarily with the province, not with the Republic as a whole. Basic identity was, as is often the case today, still felt most strongly in the home town. Van der Capellen's nationalism was also of this local kind, not even really provincial, still less nation-wide. Patriot feeling of this kind was easily united as a destructive force, but had a long way to go before it could overcome local loyalties and so perform a role that could be termed constructive.

The initial task of limiting the powers of the hereditary Stadholder was comparatively quickly and simply performed, mainly by his traditional opponents the regents of the towns of the Province of Holland. The first attack was launched against Prince Louis of Brunswick-Wolfenbüttel, who was forced to leave The Hague in 1782 and betake himself to Den Bosch where he was officially governor. A little while later the text of the Act of Consultentship was leaked to an influential German newspaper and on grounds generally to be grouped under the heading 'undue influence' (over the at the time far-from-reluctant Stadholder) Prince Louis was obliged to leave Dutch service altogether. Shortly afterwards the Stadholder and his court were ordered out of The Hague, where their life-style had been becoming more and more ostentatious, even bordering on the regal, and began to journey from one provincial residence to another, deprived of their interest in rebuilding in and around the Binnenhof in the centre of The Hague, the results of which are still plain to see today. The

[13] Kossmann 'Crisis' 165.

departure of the Court from The Hague was the sequel to William's losing his rank of Commander-in-chief, taken from him by his old opponents the anti-Stadholderian regents. All this time the *Patriotten* were building themselves into a still provincially based but becoming a more coherent and integrated body with Free Corps groups behind it and debating programmes of reform which were taking on more and more of the democratic until in June 1785 what emerged was a kind of representative system of government. A few months later a draft constitution was drawn up the principles of which bore some resemblance to those enunciated in the American Declaration of Independence.

The fourth Anglo-Dutch war ended officially only in May 1784, with the signature of the Treaty of Paris between Great Britain and the Republic. But the Republic had been included in the cease-fire which had preceded the finalizing, in January 1783, of the Treaty of Versailles between Great Britain, her colonists and her adversaries France and Spain; Dutch merchant ships had indeed become active again all through most of 1782 and in 1783. By the terms of this Paris settlement, the Republic surrendered Negapatam in Ceylon, a trading station long in dispute between the English and the Dutch East India Companies. The English company thus gained some advantage for its Sinhalese trade in that still increasingly popular commodity – Indian tea. Also English East India Company's ships were permitted to navigate freely in Far East areas from which the Dutch East India Company had endeavoured to exclude them.

It is superficially somewhat surprising to find that defeats suffered by Netherlands ships at St Eustatius or in European waters should be as it were 'compensated' by losses of territory or monopoly trading rights by the Dutch East India Company. But this company was not by this time what it had been in the earlier days. Its directors were by now quite happy to cut expenses for defence in Ceylon and to move away from an area where expansion might have been expected. The company was still sending east a fair number of vessels which returned with valuable cargoes. But there was no longer much enterprise or enthusiasm among its settled servants in the Far East. Boxer even talks of 'je m'en fiche – ism', of corruption and cynicism in the company's trading posts.[14] Moreover, it seems that contemporaries used the French 'aprés moi

[14] C. R. Boxer, *Dutch Seaborne Empire,* 291 especially authorities cited at n. 6 and 279, table showing numbers of outward bound East India men in decennia up to and including 1771–72 to 1780–81.

le déluge', as our neighbours' proverb has it, which we have taken over in deeds if not in words. The company by the end of the eighteenth century, though still sending home valuable cargoes, much moreover being sold abroad, was seemingly lacking in vitality. It was therefore convenient to draw on unrealized assets, yet another Sinhalese station which might like others in the island end up as a liability, or a monopoly (very hard and expensive to enforce) of navigation in its waterways, to buy back St Eustatius and win peace in Europe.

Final Dutch Capitulation to Foreign Influences   It is somewhat ironic to find, in the fifteen years between 1780 and 1795, that there did develop an overt and recognizable Anglo-French struggle to control the foreign policy of the Dutch Republic. Earlier, Dutch policy could still be said to be Dutch-controlled for Dutch ends. But once the débacle of the fourth Anglo-Dutch war had occurred, politics in the Republic became harder and harder to disentangle, foreign influences increased, and although more strongly expressed, specifically Dutch nationalism had less and less influence on the political scene.

We must first concern ourselves with the events leading up to the formation of yet another triangular treaty between England, the Republic and this time Prussia in place of Austria, to integrate the Dutch into a new style Ancient System of European alliances and so keep them out of the orbit of France. The architect and builder of this system was Sir James Harris, later Earl of Malmesbury, and his method of procedure was to work through the party of the Orangists. In this he was greatly assisted by the turn of events in the Netherlands in the mid-1780s.[15] It was also to Harris' advantage that the successor to Frederick the Great of Prussia, who died in August 1786, was the brother of the Princess of Orange. And moreover, the opposition to the House of Orange was even more divided than it had been before the war; not only were there divisions between the conservative, old-style regent opposition and the *Patriotten,* but the *Patriotten* during the war and after had split into nationalists, who were by now the old guard among them, and the more advanced radicals and militants. The Holland regents' Opposition, still very powerful, was aristocratic in attitudes and

[15] The English authority here is still A. Cobban, *Ambassadors and Secret Agents: The Diplomacy of the First Earl of Malmesbury at The Hague* (1945). Two English scholars, Mrs R. Gerson and Mr S. Schama, are now working in the field.

life-style; and although the intellectuals who were developing the patriot political philosophy, were sometimes also from the regenten, as a whole this section of opposition to the Stadholder was property-conscious and abhorred popular self-determination in any form other than what was traditional in the Republic. Another cause for distrust by the *Patriotten* of the common people was that especially in the province of Holland these tended to be Orangist supporters. Such divisions, between the conservative, traditional opposition to the party of the Stadholder, the more nationalist, less democratic of the *Patriotten,* and between the moderate intellectuals and the radicals, made Harris' task the easier once the extremists began to get the upper hand. Cobban is surely correct in calling the *Patriotten* 'the key to the situation' in the Republic in the 1780s.[16]

The domestic struggle in the Republic had always made itself most felt over questions of foreign policy. This was true above all for the 1780s, when the Stadholder and his party, though not by any means weak except in effective leadership, was the target for attack by both traditional regent opponents and by the Patriots. But the Patriots themselves were not at one in their aims, and again it is the situation in different provinces that has to be borne in mind. In particular, the situation in the province of Holland, where the anti-Stadholderian regents were strongest, and the urban proletariat most Orangist in sympathy, must be seen as being different from that in nearly every other province. For in Holland the Stadholder had little, if any, say in the choice of urban rulers, whereas elsewhere he had a good deal of influence in this important matter. The party situation in the Republic in the 1780s is not a simple equation of pro-French *Patriotten* being anti-Stadholderian, in alliance with the older mainly Holland province anti-Orangist regents. One has to reckon with a number of local and other influences which cut across Dutch domestic politics and make the pattern extremely confusing.

However, by 1784 the connection between domestic tension and development of Dutch foreign policy became plain once more. We should begin, it seems, with the final departure in 1782 of the Dutch garrisons from the Southern Netherlands fortresses at the request of the Emperor Joseph II. This evacuation passed off peacefully, but left behind a number of irritating questions, about property in abandoned armaments, over minor land disputes and about the

[16] *Ambassadors*, 211.

expenses of repatriating Dutch troops, even about damage done on
the march home, and about compensation for those who had built
up businesses around the supplies to the garrisons. Partly in order
to hasten the settlement of these disputes, partly in pursuit of a
desire to profit at least in part from his Southern Netherlands trade,
but also because he rebelled against accepting principles laid down
nearly a century and a half before, the Emperor Joseph II sent an
Austrian vessel into the waterways 'closed' by articles XIV and XV of
the Treaty of Munster in 1648.[17] This vessel was challenged by a
Dutch frigate, and there followed a note from the emperor asserting
that his ships must no longer be hindered from sailing waters that
bordered his territory. This assertion was followed by the so-called
tableau sommaire, a document which has been described as 'a
masterpiece in the art of bullying diplomacy'. By October 1784
diplomatic representatives had been withdrawn from The Hague
and Vienna respectively, and war was considered to be almost
inevitable.

This Scheldt crisis was not without its effect on the domestic
conflicts in the Republic. Joseph had entirely failed to understand
how strongly his assertion, that the Dutch no longer had the right to
monopolize the Scheldt waterways, would offend the nationalist
Patriots and reactivate anglophilia. Also, the Patriots not
unnaturally looked for the active support of France in the Dutch
dispute with the emperor, and looked, moreover, in vain: so that
Harris' task of restoring the hopes of the Stadholderian party in the
interests of their traditional English ally, was assisted by the whole
episode of the first attempt to re-open the Scheldt. Harris'
influence in the Republic grew stronger on the basis of reawakened
patriotism and remembered history.

Meanwhile there was developing in the Republic itself a situation
that seemed to be leading to civil war, the States of Holland versus
the Stadholder and the land-ward provinces led by Gelderland. In
September 1786, the Stadholder was deprived of his rights as
captain-general, and troops stationed outside the province of
Holland were ordered to return and to form a guard along the
boundaries of Holland and thus effectively cut off all supporters
of the Stadholder from approaching the heart-land of the Republic.
Gelderland forbade the troops stationed in the province to obey
these orders and it does seem as if especially the garrisons within the

[17] Bindoff. *Scheldt Question,* 140. For an account with somewhat contrasting
nuances, Cobban, *Ambassadors,* 49.

province were loyal to the Stadholder. But the troops were paid from the centre,[18] and money had to be found; after discussion and difficulties Harris was entrusted with a £70,000 English subsidy, the effects of which were to maintain Gelderland as an Orangist stronghold for the time being.

The danger of civil war was the greater because by the mid-1780s the Patriot Free Corps congress, which was fairly representative of such groups throughout the Republic, had voted that the event should become annual; and in the meanwhile, under Patriot and anti-Stadholderian influence combined, the Republic had actually joined with France in a defensive treaty.

We might say, then, that tendencies observable earlier, for the neutral Republic to develop on the one side a violent anti-English and anti-Stadholderian party that was sometimes pro-French, and on the other a pro-English, francophobic group around the House of Orange, had now eaten into the political life of the Republic, so dividing allegiances that civil war alone could decide the issue. But at least until after the French Revolution was well under way, France was not, and England was, able to take some steps to assist the Dutch party that favoured her rather than her adversary. English cash was now, as it had not been previously, available to assist the Orangist cause. Harris was able, by judicious use of English subsidies, to bribe the troops which had been withdrawn from the outer provinces, to neglect their task of guarding Holland, stronghold of anti-Stadholderian and Patriot opposition, against adherents of William V.

The situation in which the Orangists found themselves was particularly galling to the Princess of Orange. Hers was a dynamic personality; and to live in exile in Nijmegen, as had been her fate, and to fail to galvanize her over-acquiescent husband into activity, became unendurable. She therefore decided to take action herself, and late in June 1787 set off for The Hague accompanied only by one maid of honour and three officers, the object of her intended visit being to negotiate a settlement with the Patriots, on so reasonable a basis that to refuse her terms would be to expose them as unpatriotic demagogues. The results of this enterprise, not perhaps as desperate as might seem, in view of the conflicting attitudes among the opposition to the Stadholder, are well known. The princess was stopped by a Free Corps detachment and, by the

[18] Here we must bear in mind that the province of Holland contributed nearly 60 per cent of the revenue of the States-General.

standards of pre-French Revolution times, for a near-royal pretty roughly handled.[19] She then withdrew once more to Nijmegen; and feeling in the Republic reached a new high point. Pressure was brought to bear on the opposition to apologize to the princess, but without avail. Her brother of Prussia as well as her husband at first deplored the whole business, but presently events so fell out that Prussia invaded the Republic, the anti-Stadholderians collapsed and the Orangists returned in triumph to The Hague.

To understand how this could happen with comparative ease and within a fairly short period (Amsterdam fell to the Prussians on 10 October, and by November the government was settled and an Orangist, Van der Spiegel, installed as grand pensionary) the following considerations must be held firmly in mind. First of all, neither England nor France wanted war, and neither power was prepared to risk any outbreak to assist either side in the Republic. Both powers wanted to see an independent government functioning in the Netherlands which would still help to maintain a balance in northern Europe. A combination of Harris' skilful use of England's undercover support, and the Orange Princess's dash and daring, had produced an unexpected change of fortune for the Stadholder. But his power was still pretty incomplete, in spite of the 'happy return' of October 1787. And measures taken to ensure the loyalty of those regents who were put in power in Holland and elsewhere remained, to say the least incomplete. The restored regime was stronger than it might have been because a large number of the more radical of the Patriots fled to France, (where it used to be thought they so to say, attended a 'school of revolution'). But it was never very strong because as previously in 1747 the House of Orange was no longer able to fulfil its rôle of 'deliverer' or 'saviour'. And there was no arch-villain from whom the Republic required either deliverance or salvation, for neither France nor England were any longer aggressors.

In the following year, 1788, the external relations of the Netherlands Republic, like the domestic situation, took on a deceptive similarity to what they had been earlier, with two significant changes. For in August, the Republic made its defensive agreement with England and Prussia, which thus doubled for Austria in the earlier tri-partite treaty of 1716; and in August England and Prussia actually guaranteed the Dutch government in

[19] Cobban, *Ambassadors*, 148–50. Cobban quotes from the account in the *Annual Register* which makes amusing reading.

the traditional Stadholderian form. However the changes from earlier days were significant, because Prussia was not nearly as interested as Austria had been in protecting the Republic from French aggression before the Franco-Austrian alliances of 1756 and 1757; and the maintenance of stability in the Republic had not earlier depended as it seemed by 1788 to depend, on the preservation of the House of Orange.

The outbreak of the French Revolution naturally brought into the situation a whole range of imponderables and anxieties for the Dutch. On the other hand, international pressures were to some extent relaxed, because the major European countries were watching the progress of events in France, and England, especially in the early days of the Revolution, was anticipating being able to keep out of what was going on. The bulk of the more influential and what we could loosely call left-wing *Patriotten* were in France, and the conservative grand pensionary, Van der Spiegel, was a firm advocate of the traditional neutralist policy for the Republic. This period of 'marking time' for the Republic came to an abrupt end in the course of 1792; when France declared war in April of that year on Prussia and Austria, attempts were made to bring the Dutch into a coalition of powers to maintain a European balance against a revolutionary France, as earlier against an over-strong monarchical France. But under Van der Spiegel the Republic still remained neutral, not as yet feeling in any particular danger.

The situation changed dramatically when in November 1792 the French, whose armies had overrun almost the whole of the Southern Netherlands, ordered their commander there to take the steps needed to free navigation of the Scheldt and the Meuse. The immediate reason was to bring up reinforcements by water to lay siege to Antwerp. But there was also a desire on the part of France to establish that the closure of an international waterway was an unjustifiable limitation of natural rights. As Bindoff puts it, the opening of the navigation of the Scheldt was hastening the process by which 'the navigation . . . of international waterways would one day be placed beyond the reach of the politician in the safer hands of the international lawyer.'[20]

Opinion in the Republic was not yet, however, much inclined to accept this internationalist attitude. The ruling Stadholderians were thrown into panic, for the financial position, in spite of enhanced taxation in 1792, was very bad, the army totally insufficient to

[20] *Scheldt Question,* 143.

enforce the terms of the Treaty of Munster or to assist the various powers who from time to time, notably in 1715, had agreed to guarantee the Scheldt closure. On 21 November 1792, French ships sailed unhindered up the estuary; and on 1st February of the following year France declared war on England and on the Republic.

At first, a French invading army suffered defeat and withdrew. But as time went on those of the *Patriotten* who had remained in the Netherlands grew bolder, and were joined by returning Patriot migrants from France. Amsterdam's traditional opposition to the Stadholder was reinforced when such leading patriots as Schimmelpennick and Gogel set up there in the city a Committee for Revolution. In August renewed French attacks in Brabant met with success, Sluis, even Nijmegen, were attacked and in December French forces crossed the rivers with ease because nature this time, unlike in 1672 allied herself with the Republic's enemies and the waterways were frozen hard. By mid-January 1795 Utrecht was under siege, two days later the Stadholder and his family were on their way to England and shortly afterwards the Republic of the United Provinces came to an end.

CHAPTER NINE

Conclusion

IN the last fifteen years of its existence, the Dutch Republic was forced by external pressures, above all by those of France, to give up its chosen policy of neutrality. It was also external pressures, above all those of France, which had forced it to give up its chosen policy of neutrality in 1672. The small trading nation, eager to remain at peace with its neighbours, to continue the distribution of goods and products, and not least the distribution of ideas around the world, had not changed its ideals in the period just considered. But the conditions under which those ideals could be pursued had changed materially; and principles of non-alignment and neutrality, especially of unarmed neutrality, needed adaptation. And adaptation had been beyond the resources of a Republic suffering by the end of the eighteenth century from economic decline, governed in a fashion which looked mainly to the past, and as time went on affected by a mood of despondency amounting sometimes to despair. Van der Spiegel, when he refused to add the Republic's enfeebled strength to a proposed renewed defensive alliance between Prussia and the maritime powers (this under threat of renewed French invasion early in 1794) because he hoped to remain in touch with the enemy, was only trying to re-play under different conditions, the double game successfully carried through by his predecessor Stein in 1758. The Triple Alliance of 1788 between England, Prussia and the Republic resembled a resurrection of the contemporarily so-called 'Ancient System of European Alliances' beloved of mid-eighteenth century English Whigs, this time with Prussia playing Austria's rôle. In one way the resemblance was close, for the adversary was always France. But in 1788 the object was the *restoration* of a regime traditionally regarded as anglophile. This had not always been so; the much-maligned Princess Anna, English princess royal and gouvernante in her son's name in the 1750s, sometimes acted as much like a Dutch as an English-woman, though always as a member of the House of Orange. Hitherto, also, the opposition to the Orangists had been more Dutch in its aims than Francophile, though the powers had regarded it as pro-French. But by the 1780s its Francophilia had become plain and its patriot adherents subscribed to Enlightenment and later to French Revolutionary ideals.

But this 'plus ça change, plus c'est la même chose' air about the foreign policy of the Republic in the period between 1667 and 1795, is nonetheless deceptive. This was not so much because of changes in the Dutch political and economic situation, though changes there had been. It was due above all to the momentous change in the politics of the major European power which had been the nodal point of the Republic's foreign policy, those changes which were the result of the French Revolution in 1789. For instance the France which declared war on the Republic in 1793 was, like the France that had declared war on the Republic in 1672, actuated at least partly by ideals. In 1793 revolutionary France regarded a determination to keep the Scheldt closed in the interests of one only of the riparian powers, as an offence against the rights of man. Further, a social system like that of the Republic, in which a few rich citizens became increasingly richer, whilst the number of paupers increased annually, was regarded by the new regime in France as abhorrent. But in 1672, what had been regarded by Louis XIV as abhorrent had been the very existence of a successful, stable Republican form of government over a country which had backgrounded a near-monarchical Stadholderian family to whose ancestors it had owed so much. To Louis the treatment of the House of Orange after 1650, appeared as an affront to the whole institution of monarchy which was then so much in vogue.

More importantly, there had taken place between 1667 and 1795 a dramatic change in the ratio between the economic positions of the Republic and other European countries. This particularly affected the ability of the respective central governments to lay hands on their respective subjects' wealth and after the French Revolution the contrast between the situation in the Netherlands and in France was particularly striking. This is not the place to enter into a discussion of the causes of Dutch economic decline. But it has already been made clear that the finance of the central government in the United Provinces was dependent on prompt payment of provincial contributions, that both the province of Holland and the central government carried very heavy burdens of debt, and that Holland made a contribution of nearly 60 per cent to the total of central finance. After 1788, the province of Holland, having been virtually obliged to receive back the Stadholder, was in no hurry to contribute its quota to generality finance. Yet debt service charges were heavy and additionally as we have seen nature had shown to the Republic an unkind face in the course of the eighteenth century. The pile worm's appetite was still unsatisfied,[1] cattle plague still raged and harbours were still silting up. Worst of all, Amsterdam's entrepôt functions were less and less in demand, although backward-looking economists still urged their resuscitation.

In contrast, after the revolution in France there were court riches to be drawn on, and the revenues of nobles guillotined or in exile were also easily available to the central government, whilst early in the days of the new regime issues of paper money brought illusions of wealth. Moreover, France was now less dependent than previously on Dutch neutral shipping to bring naval stores to her dockyards or to get home her colonial produce. Scandinavian neutrals had by now increased the numbers of their merchant men and were taking over from the Dutch, whose ships were no longer the largest or the most efficient in Europe and whose carrying trade was thus no longer indispensable.

[1] As indeed still today. The Delta works have been found to be thus affected recently.

Government instability was also very marked in the last fifteen years of the Republic. Divisions, upheaval, a restoration by force of a discredited regime by foreign powers, followed by seven years of dependence on England and Prussia – what a fall from the proud days of the previous century! But less than two decades after the last hereditary Stadholder had fled ignominiously in the face of French invasion, it proved possible to set up in the House of Orange a constitutional monarchy 'the unitary shape' of which was never seriously contested.[2] The hereditary Stadholderate, in spite of its formality and extravagance, its so-exclusive turning in on itself, played some part in breaking down provincialism and in bringing in to the centre of government the so-called six allies of the province of Holland,[3] reminding us all that neither before nor after 1795 has Holland been a synonym for the Netherlands.

This account of Dutch foreign policy between 1667 and 1795 is the story of the long continuance but ultimate failure of a determination to remain unaligned and neutral in a Europe that would often have liked somehow to make use of the Republic for its own ends. Dutch foreign policy in this period was designed to keep the Republic independent of European power blocks, and to allow it to mind its own business of acting as a distribution point and centre of communications between north and south, between east and west. Admittedly its emergence in this rôle was partly fortuitous, for Europe at this time was intent on immediate emergencies and no great power was free to rival this small state, which was not too well equipped by nature for so vital a rôle. But having developed its facilities and the necessary expertise the Republic could and did exist for many years, flanked by weakened Spain to the south, and rival German princelings to the east, growing rich on the proceeds of entrepôt trade. When France became aggressive, the situation changed, defensive measures had to be taken and alliances made. Once the danger from monarchical France subsided, defence and alliances came to look unnecessary; the Dutch could agree with their French adversaries by means of neutral trading services. But French recrudescence under a new government, with ideas allied to those of Dutch intellectuals and social reformers, caught the Dutch government unawares; and the result was the débâcle of 1795.

---

[2] Kossmann, 'Crisis', 156.

[3] H.Wansink, 'Holland and Six Allies' in *Britain and The Netherlands* IV, eds. Bromley and Kossman, 133–55.

Bibliography

It is now becoming somewhat easier for non-Dutch readers to keep up with the findings of Dutch historians. Two series designed to this end are now available and will, hopefully, continue. There are the *Acta Historiae Neerlandicae,* previously *Neerlandica* and published in English, French or German, but now including Belgium and appearing in English, which contain translations of important articles by Netherlands historians, and summaries of significant works. Volume VI, published in 1973, contains what will be a continuing feature, a review article devoted to recent Dutch and Belgian historical publications. Also now published are 4 volumes of papers read to Anglo-Dutch historical conferences, and a fifth is in preparation. These volumes are edited by J. S. Bromley and E. H. Kossmann and will from now on be published, as will the *Acta,* by Nijhoff in The Hague. Moreover, recent Dutch doctoral dissertations, often the fruits of ten to twenty years' research, have statutorily to include a summary in English, French or German, but usually in English. Some publications by established Dutch historians, particularly specialist monographs, also provide conclusions in one of these languages.

There are also writings in English by Dutchmen, and translations of Dutch historical works into English. Particularly useful for this short study are two articles by E. H. Kossmann in the *New Cambridge Modern History* IV, ed. J. P. Cooper (Cambridge, 1970), V, ed. F. L. Carsten (Cambridge, 1961), and one by A. Veenendaal in VI, ed. J. S. Bromley (Cambridge, 1970). Volume VII, ed. J. O. Lindsay (Cambridge, 1957) is not now so useful. There is also a Dutch source publication in several volumes, *Archives de la Maison d'Orange Nassau,* under the general editorship of Groen van Prinsterer. Much of this material, including the introductions to the three relevant series, 3, 4 and 5, and the co-ordinating volume, is in French. But these documents, because of their Orangist source, do not give a balanced view of Dutch policy as a whole, a fact sometimes overlooked by non-Dutch historians. P. C. Geyl's 2-volume history of the Republic in its Golden Age has appeared in English as *The Netherlands in the Seventeenth Century* (1936 and 1964) as has his *Oranje en Stuart (Orange and Stuart)* (1970).

In the following short list of 44 works in English or French, and 8 in Dutch, which have been found particularly useful in completing this short study, it will be noted that most deal with the seventeenth century. This relates to English historian's tendencies to ignore the Republic once it ceased to play an active part in Europe, and to Dutch historians' disinclination to concern themselves with what is regarded as an inglorious period. Such Dutch titles as are included in the list, out of a large number consulted, are present because the information they contain is virtually unobtainable elsewhere.

Books in English

P. W. Bamford, *Forests and French Sea Power* (Toronto, 1956)
Violet Barbour, *Capitalism in Amsterdam* (Baltimore, 1950)
S. B. Baxter, *William III* (1966)
S. T. Bindoff, *The Scheldt Question* (London, 1945)
C. R. Boxer, *The Dutch Seaborne Empire* (1965)
Alice Clare Carter, *The Dutch Republic in Europe in the Seven Years War* (1971)
G. N. Clark, *The Dutch Alliance and the War against French Trade* (Manchester, 1923)
P. G. M. Dickson, *The Financial Revolution in England* (1967)
R. Geike and I. A. Montgomery, *The Dutch Barrier* (Cambridge, 1930)
P. Geyl, *The Netherlands in the Seventeenth Century* I and II (1936 and 1964)
P. Geyl, *Orange and Stuart* (1970)
A. Goslinga, *Slingelandt's Efforts towards European Peace* (The Hague, 1915)
R. M. Hatton, *Diplomatic Relations between Great Britain and The Netherlands, 1714–1721* (1950)
K. H. Haley, *The Dutch in the Seventeenth Century* (1972)
J. Huizinga, *Dutch Civilization in the Seventeenth Century* (1968)
J. R. Jones, *Britain and Europe in the Seventeenth Century* (1966) (Foundations of Modern History)
A. M. Lambert, *The Making of the Dutch Landscape* (1971)
Isable de Madariaga, *Britain, Russia and the Armed Neutrality of 1780* (Oxford, 1938)
J. K. Oudendijk, *Status and Extent of Adjacent Waters: A Historical Orientation* (Leiden, 1970)
R. Pares, *Colonial Blockade and Neutral Rights, 1739–1763* (Oxford, 1938)
G. J. Renier, *William of Orange* (Short Bibliographies no. 24, 1932) *The Dutch Nation* (1944)
H. H. Rowen (ed.), *The Low Countries in early modern times* (London, 1972) (Documentary History of Western Civilisation)
H. H. Rowen, *The Ambassador Prepares for War: The Dutch Embassy of Arnauld de Pomponne, 1669–1671* (The Hague, 1957)
K. W. Swart, *The Sale of Offices in the Seventeenth Century* (The Hague, 1949)
William Temple, *Works* (4 vols., 1757) esp. vol I
A. McC. Wilson, *French Foreign Policy during the administration of Cardinal Fleury, 1726–1743,* Harvard Historical Studies XL (Cambridge, 1936)
Charles Wilson, *Anglo-Dutch commerce and finance in the Eighteenth Century* (Cambridge, 1941)
Charles Wilson, *The Dutch Republic and the civilisation of the Seventeenth Century* (1968)

g: common

Alice Clare Carter, 'How to revise treaties without negotiating: common sense, mutual tears and the Anglo-Dutch trade disputes of 1759, in *Studies in Diplomatic History,* eds. R. M. Hatton and M. S. Anderson, (1970)

D. J. Roorda, 'The Ruling Classes in Holland in the Seventeenth Century', in *Britain and the Netherlands* II, eds. J. S. Bromley and E. H. Kossmann, (Groningen, 1964)

Jerker Rosen, 'Scandinavia and the Baltic', in *New Cambridge Modern History* VI, ed. F. L. Carsten, (Cambridge, 1961)

H. H. Rowen, 'John de Witt and the Triple Alliance', *Journal of Modern History* XVII (1954) with long list of citations at n. 1

J. W. Smit, 'The Netherlands and Europe in the Seventeenth and Eighteenth centuries', in *Britain and the Netherlands in Europe and Asia,* eds. J. S. Bromley and E. H. Kossmann, (1968)

J. G. Stork-Penning, 'The ordeal of the States – some remarks on Dutch politics during the war of the Spanish Succession', *Acta Historiae Neerlandica* II

H. Wansink, 'Holland and six allies', in *Britain and the Netherlands* IV, eds. J. S. Bromley and E. H. Kossmann, (The Hague, 1971)

Charles Wilson and A. C. Carter, 'Dutch Investment in Eighteenth Century England. A Note on Yardsticks' and 'Note on A Note on Yardsticks', *The Economic History Review* 2nd series, XII, No. 3, (1960)

Charles Wilson, 'Taxation and the decline of empires: an unfashionable theme', *Economic History and the Historian* (1969)

G. Zeller, 'French Diplomacy and foreign policy', in *New Cambridge Modern History* V, ed. F. L. Carsten, (Cambridge, 1961)

Books in French

L. André et E. Bourgeois, *Recueil des Instructions données aux ambassadeurs de France. Hollande* III (Paris, 1926)

N. Laude, *La Compagnie d'Ostende et son activité coloniale au Bengale 1725–1730* (Bruxelles, 1944)

Books in Dutch

J. S. Bartstra, *Vlootherstel en legeraugmentatie* (Assen, 1952)

J. G. van Dillen, *Van Rijkdom en Regenten* (Amsterdam, 1970)

S. J. Fockema Andrae, *De Nederlandse Staat onder de Republiek* (3rd edition, Amsterdam, 1969)

P. Geyl, *Revolutiedagen to Amsterdam* (The Hague, 1936)

P. Geyl, *Willem IVde en Engeland tot 1748* (The Hague, 1924)

D. Houtzager, *Hollands lijf en losrentingen voor 1672* (Schiedam, 1950)

N. Japikse, *De Geschiedenis van het Huis van Oranje-Nassau* (2 vols., The Hague, 1938) with genealogical tables

Joh. de Vries, *De Economische achteruitgang der republiek in the achttiende eeuw* (Amsterdam, 1959)

Index